Praise for *Help Them Grow or Watch Them Go*

"Deceptively simple. Absolutely relevant. Bev
opment and give managers the key to unlock
—**Heidi Brandow, Director, Global Learning and**

T0268364

"Life and business are all about where you pa
growth of your people . . . and they will grow your business. The authors do a
great job in spelling out the how-tos!"
—**Chip Conley, author of *Wisdom@Work* and Strategic Advisor for Hospitality and
Leadership, Airbnb**

"This edition takes us into the realities of today's business landscape and shows
that if we want to grow our business, we have to grow our people. It walks
the reader through career conversations in a way that isn't overwhelming and
rather focuses on leaders being genuine and having meaningful conversations."
—**Robin Cerrati, Vice President, Human Resources, Compass Group**

"Should be the career conversation bible for busy leaders!"
—**Marshall Goldsmith, author of the *New York Times* bestseller *Triggers* and
coauthor of *How Women Rise***

"Organizations in Asia need to take career development initiatives seriously, and
managers need to be supported with simple skills and tools to build trust and
overcome cultural barriers. This book offers an approach to career development that works cross-culturally and enables companies in Asia to deal more
effectively with this talent management challenge."
—**Tan Siew Inn, Founding Partner, The Flame Centre, Singapore, and author of
*Wholeness in a Disruptive World***

"*Help Them Grow or Watch Them Go* is an important contribution to leading
organizations where people and talent growth matters to success."
—**Kevin Wilde, Executive Leadership Fellow, Carlson School of Management**

"In all my years coaching executives on career development, this is the best
and most comprehensive resource available. It takes the complex issue of
career development and simplifies it with real, action-oriented tips, tools,
and insights. It's relevant for new supervisors, senior executives, and HR
professionals at any level in any industry."
—**Sharon Silverman, Senior Vice President, Talent Acquisition, Gingerfinds**

"At last, a hands-on book that's smart, practical, and honest. Everyone knows
that people make all the difference; this book will teach you how to make a
difference with your people."
—**Alan Webber, cofounder of *Fast Company*, author of *Rules of Thumb*, and Mayor
of Santa Fe, New Mexico**

"Improving the skills of our workforce is one of the country's most important economic challenges. It has to start with employers, and *Help Them Grow or Watch Them Go* tells you how to do it painlessly."

—**Peter Cappelli, Director, Center for Human Resources, The Wharton School, and Professor of Management, University of Pennsylvania**

"Great read for those who want to help individuals develop. It is full of useful materials that are easy to access. Ideal for a manager who wants to learn about coaching others."

—**Edward E. Lawler III, Distinguished Professor of Business, Marshall School of Business, University of Southern California, and coauthor of *Management Reset***

"Improving retention and building engagement are the driving factors for the talent development strategy of the Hearst Capital Management group. We're implementing *Help Them Grow* concepts because they provide managers and employees with an easy-to-follow yet impactful framework for career conversations. Through career conversations, we're increasing engagement and, more importantly, supporting our employees' careers."

—**Heather Ragone, Senior Director, Talent Development, Hearst**

"Ingersoll Rand's focus on development is improving year over year. Our leaders don't just coach for performance, they coach for development. How does best-in-class engagement and employee retention sound to you? Does an organization filled with career coaches sound interesting? Read this book!"

—**Craig Mundy, Vice President, Human Resources, Strategic Business Units, Ingersoll Rand**

"*Help Them Grow or Watch Them Go* provides a practical road map for managers who know that they want to help their teams but may not know the clear, specific steps they can take. Managers, employees, and the organizations they serve will benefit from the wisdom in this book."

—**Rebecca L. Ray, PhD, Executive Vice President, Human Capital, The Conference Board**

"I loved this book. Draw from the abundant list of simple yet powerful questions and become the best talent manager in your organization."

—**Tina Sung, Vice President, Government Transformation and Agency Partnerships, Partnership for Public Service**

"A great guidebook for those whose job it is to help other people grow, with all the right questions we need to be asking!"

—**Frances Hesselbein, President and CEO, The Frances Hesselbein Leadership Institute**

Help Them **Grow** or Watch Them **Go**

HELP THEM

THIRD EDITION

Updated and Expanded

GROW
or WATCH
THEM
GO

Career Conversations
Organizations Need
and Employees *Still* Want

Beverly Kaye and
Julie Winkle Giulioni

BK

Berrett–Koehler Publishers, Inc.
a BK Business book

Berrett-Koehler Publishers, Inc., 1333 Broadway, Suite 1000, Oakland, CA 94612-1921,
Tel: (510) 817-2277; Fax: (510) 817-2278; www.bkconnection.com

Ordering Information

Quantity sales. Special discounts are available on quantity purchases by corporations, associations, and others. For details, contact the "Special Sales Department" at the Berrett-Koehler address above.

Individual sales. Berrett-Koehler publications are available through most bookstores. They can also be ordered directly from Berrett-Koehler: Tel: (800) 929-2929; Fax: (802) 864-7626; www.bk connection.com.

Orders for college textbook/course adoption use. Please contact Berrett-Koehler: Tel: (800) 929-2929; Fax: (802) 864-7626.

Distributed to the U.S. trade and internationally by Penguin Random House Publisher Services. Berrett-Koehler and the BK logo are registered trademarks of Berrett-Koehler Publishers, Inc.

Printed in Canada

Berrett-Koehler books are printed on long-lasting acid-free paper. When it is available, we choose paper that has been manufactured by environmentally responsible processes. These may include using trees grown in sustainable forests, incorporating recycled paper, minimizing chlorine in bleaching, or recycling the energy produced at the paper mill.

Library of Congress Cataloging in Publication
  Names: Kaye, Beverly, 1943– author. | Giulioni, Julie Winkle, author.
  Title: Help them grow or watch them go : career conversations organizations need and employees
    still want / Beverly Kaye, Julie Winkle Giulioni.
  Description: Third edition. | Oakland, CA : Berrett-Koehler Publishers, [2024] | Revised edition of
    the authors' Help them grow or watch them go, [2019]
  Identifiers: LCCN 2024010432 (print) | LCCN 2024010433 (ebook) | ISBN 9798890570253
    (paperback) | ISBN 9798890570260 (pdf) | ISBN 9798890570277 (epub)
  Subjects: LCSH: Career development.
  Classification: LCC HF5549.5.C35 K39 2024 (print) | LCC HF5549.5.C35 (ebook) | DDC
    658.3/124—dc23/eng/20240311
  LC record available at https://lccn.loc.gov/2024010432
  LC ebook record available at https://lccn.loc.gov/2024010433

Third Edition

32 31 30 29 28 27 26 25 24 | 10 9 8 7 6 5 4 3 2 1

Book produced by BookMatters, cover and text designed by Ashley Ingram based on a design by Nancy Austin.

From Julie,

To Peter, for knowing I could do this—and making sure I did... yet again.

To Nick, Jenna, Diane, and Bailey, for the constant joy and lessons learned from watching you all grow.

From Beverly,

To Barry, for truly being the wind beneath my wings.

To Lindsey and Jill, for showing me love in every single interaction.

CONTENTS

INTRODUCTION

YOU CAN'T SAY WE DIDN'T WARN YOU

Since publishing the first edition of *Help Them Grow or Watch Them Go* in 2012, we've been preaching the career development gospel. Through our writing, speaking, and training, we've connected with hundreds of thousands of leaders who want to give their employees a better experience of growth—and give their organizations the benefits that come along with it. Yet it was the perfect storm created by the global pandemic and the ensuing economic crisis that has delivered our message to the world more powerfully than our words ever could.

The past several years have served as a compelling case study of the nonnegotiable nature of career development, yielding a cautionary (and pithy) message for organizations and leaders:

Help them grow or watch them go!

Recent events have been a wake-up call. Discussions of attrition on the nightly news and at the kitchen table. Wide-scale business closures. The profound effects we've felt as consumers. Countless studies linking lack of growth and opportunity to talent migration—some of you may have changed jobs yourselves for this reason. This all adds up to a visceral experience and understanding of workforce dynamics and the key role that development plays.

But let's face it. While the disruptions may be more dramatic this time around, it's not the first time we've seen economic and labor market dynamics conspire to amplify the importance of development. The pendulum is always in flux. Too frequently, though, we've responded to tough times with a recommitment to employees and their growth in the moment. Then our short attention spans and memories are turned to something else... until the next employment-related crisis.

What IF ...

▶ we learned the lesson this time?

▶ organizations and leaders found a sustainable way to maintain a focus on and commitment to development—during good times and bad?

▶ career development was the reason people stayed rather than left an organization?

- -

We can. They can. And it can be. That's why we've updated this book... again.

HELP THEM gROW

As a result of our contemporary appreciation for the value of growth and its outsized effect on retention, career development has only taken on greater importance since we first wrote this book. In today's business environment, talent is still the major differentiator and is increasingly viewed as a competitive advantage. As artificial intelligence and other advances take hold, we're coming to terms with the reality that there's no substitute for what human beings are uniquely suited to contribute to the workplace. As a result, developing people to optimize their capacity has become a compelling and strategic priority across organizations.

Beyond its retention implications, developing talent continues to be recognized as one of the most significant drivers of employee engagement, which in turn is the key to the business outcomes you seek:

revenue, profitability, innovation, productivity, customer loyalty, quality, cycle time reduction, and more—everything organizations need to
survive and thrive.

In another perfect storm, employees are expressing a desire for
development at exactly the time that organizations need that growth
most. The predictions related to workforce readiness in the years to
come are dire. Today's skills fall woefully short of meeting tomorrow's
needs. Without significant upskilling and reskilling, a frightening per-
centage of employees will find themselves and their ability to contribute irrelevant.

At the same time, the reality of career development continues to
morph in response to the evolving business landscape. Boomers are living longer—and in some sectors working longer. Belt-tightening efforts
that led to delayering and downsizing show no signs of loosening and
may even accelerate. There are fewer and fewer levels of leadership to
which to aspire. Work gets organized and done more organically these
days. More jobs are being filled with contingent and contract workers.
All of this can breed a sense of scarcity and leave the impression that
there aren't as many opportunities as there once were.

Career development can no longer be treated as a "nice to do"
or "when you get around to it" perk. Today helping others grow has
become a mission-critical priority.

OR WATCH THEM *GO*

"Ignore the development imperative at your own peril." Who would
have guessed that this line from our last edition would have foreshad-
owed events to come? The dynamics driving the Great Resignation,
responsible for wreaking havoc on so many organizations, are still
with us today, albeit on a lesser scale. Everyday employees who believe
that their careers are not getting the attention they deserve make the
decision to leave. Some resign to pursue employment in organizations
that offer greater opportunity for growth and learning. Others decide

the flexibility of freelance life fits them better, and they cobble together a variety of projects that become their career.

But an equally dangerous group is made up of those who stay but withdraw their engagement, motivation, and enthusiasm for the work. Remember quiet quitting? It remains alive and well—perhaps not-so-quietly undermining team dynamics, effectiveness, and results.

A word to the wise: This dynamic is not reserved for tight labor market cycles. The pendulum is going to swing back and forth. And whether it favors the employer or employee, you'll always have competition for top talent—the performers your organization needs. Career development is still your greatest weapon—whether it's a war or just a tiff for talent that you're facing.

THE "THEM" IN HELP THEM GROW: WHO ARE THEY?

When we wrote the first edition of this book in 2012, we loosely used the word *employee* to refer to the bulk of the people who work for you. Fast-forward to today, and you're managing a complex talent ecosystem of resources. Sure, you have your full-time workforce, but you likely also lead part-time employees, project team members, contractors, consultants, interns, and more. Gig workers are also a significant economic and employment factor.

As the number of these nontraditional contributors grows, organizations and leaders are grappling with hard questions around effectiveness, access to development, resource allocation, and equity issues. Let us offer a simple and proactive solution: Help them all grow! It's time to take a more generous and democratic approach to growth. We know what you're thinking:

► Yes, gig workers may not be with you for long.

► Yes, the contingent workforce will build skills that they may pack up and take elsewhere.

► Yes, the same is true of your full-timers.

No longer are there lifetime employment guarantees or gold watches. You know it and so does your workforce. Today they're looking for other sources of security—skills, knowledge, and experiences. Offer these and—although there's no guarantee that people will stay longer—they'll be able to contribute more while they're with you. And you'll build an attractive employment brand in a competitive marketplace.

We'll still use the word *employee* throughout this book, but we strongly suggest that you read it as *everybody* and apply these ideas to the full range of people—regardless of employment status—with whom you work.

CAREER CONVERSATIONS ORGANIZATIONS NEED AND EMPLOYEES *STILL* WANT

So what's a leader to do? Plenty. And it might be easier than you expect.

Quality career development boils down to quality **conversations**.

Quality career development still boils down to quality conversations.

Throughout this book, we'll challenge you to reframe career development in such a way that responsibility rests squarely with the employee, allowing your role to be more about prompting, guiding, reflecting, exploring ideas, activating enthusiasm, and driving action. This means talking about rather than actually doing the heavy lifting of development.

We'll offer a framework for thinking about conversations that help others grow. It involves three distinct types of conversations: hindsight, foresight, and insight.

▶ Hindsight conversations help others look backward and inward to determine who they are, where they've been, what they love, and where they excel. Chapters 3 and 4 provide questions and ideas for helping others look back as a basis for moving forward.

▶ Foresight conversations are designed to keep employees looking forward and outward toward changes, trends, and the ever-evolving big picture. Chapter 5 offers easy-to-use, straightforward tools that are long on value and short on your time investment.

▶ Leveraging the insights that surface from the convergence of hindsight and foresight is the focus of Chapters 6, 7, and 8. Where are there opportunities to carve out a space to grow and perform? How can we help others update their definitions of career success? Of the work that needs to be done, which activities will give people unique experiences and fodder for development? These are just some of the questions we'll take on in these chapters.

▶ But how can you make all of this happen at the speed of business? Chapter 9 outlines how to grow with the flow or embed development into everyday life through heightened awareness and fluid conversation strategies.

▶ In Chapter 10 we'll explore how to make all of this happen within the more challenging context of remote and hybrid working arrangements.

HOW TO READ THIS BOOK

You're probably doing a pretty good job so far. Here are a few thoughts to get the most from the experience.

This book was written for anyone who has a role in developing others. The titles vary from organization to organization: supervisor, manager, director, team lead, project leader, vice president, CEO. Seasoned executives to first-time frontline leaders. Line and staff personnel. For-profit and nonprofit leaders. Small business owners. Readers have told us that the ideas we share apply equally well at home to the very human domain of parenting and even life in general.

We've chosen to use the term *leader* generically. Whenever you see it, *leader* means you.

This book is all about the career conversations employees still want. So we'll draw heavily upon the employee's voice. These are real individuals in the workplace whose eloquent insights make the point far better than we could. They aren't entitled whiners with unrealistic expectations. They're your solid citizens. The ones you count on to produce. The ones you're hoping will stick around.

▶ TRY THIS

Throughout the book, you'll find lots of questions and activities you can use with your employees. We'll call them out like this. Have an upcoming career conversation? Scan the pages for an exercise, tuck the book under your arm, and you're ready to go.

WHAT ABOUT YOU?

You're somebody's employee too, right? And if you're like many managers, you get caught in the middle, doing the right thing for your employees but not necessarily having it done for you. As you read this book, you may find yourself thinking, *This sounds pretty good, but what about me?* Answer: do it yourself—do it for yourself! At least one time in each chapter, we'll turn the table and ask, "What about you?"

And keep in mind that the tools and questions throughout this book are highly flexible. Change *you* to *I*, and you're ready for some self-discovery. You might find it helpful to review the answers with someone at work or at home. Fresh eyes may pick up clues and offer a different perspective and new insights. Bottom line: as you invest in building skills to support your employees' development, don't be afraid to be selfish and apply what you're learning to yourself and your own career as well. You'll become a better career coach if you do.

We'll close each chapter with some what-ifs. We know that as a leader who's responsible for delivering business results, you must keep your feet planted firmly on the ground. So from that grounded position, take a moment to consider what just might be possible.

What IF...

▶ you kept reading and tried out even one or two ideas from each chapter with your employees?

- -

They would **grow.**

Develop Me or I'm **HISTORY**!

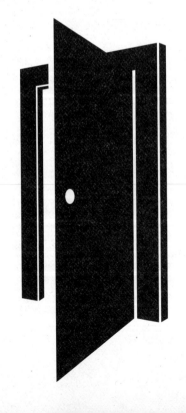

Spending forty-sixty-eighty hours somewhere each week...I want it to mean something. I want to feel like I'm moving forward somehow. If I can't grow here, I've gotta look elsewhere.

—An employee (perhaps yours)

The decision to assume a leadership role in today's workplace comes with a front-row seat to some of the greatest business challenges of our time. Day in and day out, you must:

Do exponentially more with infinitely less. It's become cliché, but this reality permeates life at work as the vise continues to tighten—including around talent in many sectors. You've likely become a master at elevating quality while at the same time finding ways to reduce costs, time, and other resources below levels you ever imagined were possible. And the reward? Do even more with even less.

Navigate extraordinary levels of change, uncertainty, and complexity. The unknowns outnumber the knowns today. Yet others look to you for clarity and direction in an increasingly unpredictable environment. But it's not just business matters that are challenging. People matters are as well. Recent events have left many employees feeling uneasy and insecure. Add to that unprecedented levels of stress, anxiety, and burnout, and leaders are now in the complicated position of managing a mental health crisis.

Meet ever-expanding expectations. Every quarter, you're asked to do a little (or a lot) more. Bigger sales. Greater numbers of service interactions. More projects. Higher scores. Beyond stakeholders and executives, employees are expressing greater expectations as well. Today's employees are not shy about sharing their desire for a different relationship with work—one that offers more meaning, flexibility, balance, and learning. And they're holding their employers to new standards around social responsibility, justice, and other matters formerly not the domain of the workplace.

Deliver the next big thing. Most organizations believe that if they're not moving forward, they're sliding backward. Innovation gets its picture on business magazine covers because it represents the promise of greater success. Disruption (especially in the form of digital transformation and AI) is the name of the game, altering the job landscape—eliminating some roles, adding others, and promising to change the complexion of work for most of us in the years to come.

Engage the most diverse workforce in history. Never have we had more richness at work. But with that richness has come challenges with inclusion, equity, and belonging. When you add "hybrid" and "remote" to the list of demographic factors that define (and too often divide) us, then leaders must also grapple with creating authentic connection among and with workers who no longer operate in shared space and time.

Future-proof the workforce. In the face of today's accelerated change, the half-life of skills is quickly shrinking, threatening to render a significant portion of the workforce ill prepared (at best) or totally irrelevant (at worst) when it comes to meeting the challenges of future work. As a result, you're charged with upskilling, reskilling, and pre-skilling employees at a pace and on a scale never imagined.

And, no matter how long, hard, or smart you work, you can't do all of this alone. Success depends upon tapping the talents, strengths, and skills that everyone has to offer. (By *everyone*, remember, we're not just talking about full-time employees—the workforce has dramatically grown to include gig workers, contingent support, contractors and consultants, interns, and even externs.) So today, your success rests upon finding ways to continually expand everyone's capacity, engagement, and ability to contribute to the organization.

Our decades of experience working with hundreds of best-in-class leaders—those who consistently develop the most capable, flexible, and engaged teams able to drive exceptional business results—reveals that they all share one quality: they make career development a priority and a regular habit.

Career development is among the most frequently **forgotten** tool for driving business **results**…

yet

it's completely within a leader's sphere of **influence**.

A "HISTORY" LESSON

Even during challenging economic times, your best and brightest have options. Failing to help employees grow can lead them to resign and take their talents elsewhere. They become "history." But what can be equally damaging as this talent drain are the employees who stay, quietly quitting and becoming increasingly disengaged. Their bodies show up for work every day, but their commitment has moved on.

So, if career development is a tool that can deliver what organizations need most—productivity gains, expense reduction, retention, quality improvements, innovation, and bottom-line results—why isn't everyone using it?

DEFINING TERMS

Perhaps it's frequently forgotten because the term *career development* strikes fear into many leaders' hearts.

WHAT ABOUT YOU?

Take a moment to think about what career development means to you. What's involved? What's your role?

Whatever your answer, we'll bet that ours is simpler. You see, many leaders are intimidated by or steer clear of career development because they have a mistaken, outdated, or overwhelming definition of the term. So try this definition on for size:

Career development is nothing more than **helping others grow.** And nothing less.

Helping others grow can take a nearly unlimited number of forms. On one end of the continuum, you help employees prepare for and move to new or expanded roles in obvious and visible ways. But far more frequently, growth shows up on the other end of the continuum, in small, subtle ways that quietly create greater challenge, interest, and satisfaction in a job.

The problem is that too often career development evokes images of forms, checklists, and deadlines. And let's be honest—the organization needs you to comply with these processes and systems to support important human resources, manpower, and succession planning work. But administrative compliance with paperwork and processes is *not* career development. Unfortunately, these artifacts too frequently overshadow the true art of development.

Genuine, meaningful, and sustainable career development occurs through the human act of conversation.

Whether it's a formal individual development planning (IDP) meeting or an on-the-fly connection, it's the quality of the conversation that matters most to employees. That's how they judge *your* performance and *their* development. And if they decide you're not helping them grow, they'll make the decision to go—physically, emotionally, or both.

AI VERSUS HI

Love it or hate it, artificial intelligence is here to stay—and changing the way work gets done in both subtle and profound ways. It's a powerful tool that has the potential to further democratize and personalize the experience of learning and development for employees. Greater access to opportunities across the entire organization versus the narrow selection of what might be available within one's department or silo. Targeted interventions that really deliver on the promise of "just-for-me" and "just-in-time" versus generic "come one, come all" programming. On-demand coaching for addressing tough career development challenges versus waiting for the next scheduled conversation.

Future generations will look back on this period as a renaissance of growth. But this golden age is not the exclusive domain of technology. Leaders will continue to play a vital role because

AI (artificial intelligence) is no match for HI (human interaction).

The digital recommendations, options, and guidance that are currently available—and that will only become more sophisticated, nuanced, and helpful over time—are important but incomplete inputs to the process of growth. Human interaction is required for people to make the most of these rich resources and use them to develop and grow. After all, it's humans rather than bots who are uniquely suited to help someone

- ► See themselves, their talents, and their potential as others see them
- ► Build contextual understanding so they can navigate the political and cultural landscape
- ► Feel safe enough to take risks and try something new
- ► Facilitate relationship building that will support success
- ► Enhance visibility through advocacy efforts
- ► Process experiences and translate them into learning
- ► Feel heard, seen, and genuinely valued by the leader and the organization

So take advantage of every digital tool available to support the growth of your employees. But know that genuine development is prompted less through AI queries and more though the HI that you, as a human, are uniquely suited to offer.

Careers are developed **one conversation** at a time…

over time.

IMMOBILIZING MYTHS

So, if it really is as simple as just talking to people, why isn't career development a more common feature of the organizational landscape?

Over the years, leaders—by sharing oral history and spinning lore—have created and continue to propagate several myths. And these myths or beliefs keep them from having the very career conversations their employees want. Which are familiar to you?

Myth 1—There isn't enough time.

> No one will argue that time is among the scarcest resources available to leaders today. But let's get real. You're having conversations already—probably all day long. What if you could redirect some of that time and redeploy some of those conversations to focus on careers and development?

Myth 2—I can't give them what they want.

> This myth is based upon the assumption that everyone wants more, bigger, or better—things like promotions, raises, prestige, power. If you believe this, you likely view career development as a confounding no-win situation. Since these things you imagine others want are in woefully short supply, it's understandable that many leaders might avoid a potentially disappointing and demoralizing conversation. But based on our research, the fundamental assumption behind this response is patently inaccurate. Today's employees are looking for a different relationship with work—one that depends less upon the traditional trappings of career development and more on the experience of meaning, purpose, flexibility, challenge, balance, and more—all things a leader can help facilitate.

Myth 3—Why rock the boat?

> If I don't talk about it, they may not think about it. Developing people increases the likelihood that they'll leave and upset the balance

of your well-running department, right? Wrong. Employees have growth on their minds—whether you address it or not. Withholding these conversations is a greater danger to the status quo than engaging in them.

Myth 4—Employees are responsible for their careers.

Employees must own the development of their careers. Full stop. If they're not in the driver's seat, the vehicle isn't going anywhere. But that doesn't mean that leaders are off the hook. You have an essential role as navigational support, helping others steer their career development toward success. And that role plays out in large part through conversation.

Myth 5—The learning and development professionals will take care of that.

Organization-sponsored training is a rich and valuable resource. And considering the urgent skills shortages facing many organizations, assigning an employee to a workshop or webinar could be an essential next step. But formal programs are just the tip of the iceberg. Informal opportunities and growth experiences within the workflow abound. Whether formal or informal, though, don't be lulled into thinking that your obligation is satisfied once the activity is assigned. Your partnership throughout the process will help employees turn learning into actionable career development.

If you're like most leaders, a few of these myths likely resonate with you. Dog-ear or bookmark this page and come back to it after you've completed the book. We predict that when you are introduced to a different way of looking at your role, you may also look at career development and these myths a little differently.

But, until then, remember this: growing the business means growing people. Forget that—and the rest is history.

What IF...

► you reframed and expanded how you think about career development?

► the business challenges leaders face could actually provide opportunities for growth?

► leaders could break through the myths that undermine their success
and their employees' growth?

- -

— 2 —

Can
We
TALK?

I'm realistic. I know your time is tight and you've got lots of other priorities. My career probably isn't at the top of your list. Don't worry—I've gotten the message that I own my career. I just need a thinking partner who'll help me step back every once in a while and focus on my development.

—An employee (perhaps yours)

If you're like most leaders, you care. You've become accustomed to taking on more and more, expanding your job description with countless "other duties as assigned"—and even some that aren't. Developing the careers of the people who report to you is on a growing (read: crushing) list of to-dos.

What if you could reimagine your role around helping others grow? What if you reframed this task (which, let's face it, gets put on the back burner much of the time anyway) in such a way that employees are the star of their career development story? What if yours became a supporting role with a focus on prompting, guiding, reflecting, exploring ideas, activating enthusiasm, and enabling action rather than actually doing all the work?

Guess what? That's how it should be. And that's how you help people own their careers. That's also how you can fit career development into your already full day.

Somehow the simple human act of helping people grow has gotten very complicated—processes on top of checklists with references to resource guides—and the to-do list keeps growing. Is it any wonder that you want to steer clear?

But here's our promise to you. Career development is much simpler than all that.

I got tired of orchestrating development experiences for people who just blew them off like they were nothing. I finally saw that the gift of heavy lifting I was giving my people was not appreciated. If I owned their development plans, they didn't. So I backed way off. Now I'm totally there for them, will talk it all out, explore possibilities, help them think it through. But when it comes to making it happen, they've got to take the lead. That's their job.

—Manager, logistics

For years we've heard that talk is cheap. Not true.

Astute managers have gotten comfortable with talking more and doing less. These are no slugs—they're strategists. They appreciate the power of conversations to inspire and generate change in others.

Conversation has the power to touch employees' hearts and minds more deeply than the well-intentioned steps you might take on someone else's behalf. You need nothing more than your own words to inspire reflection and commitment. From that can spring actions that employees own, actions that will help them realize their personal definitions of success.

"The action is in the interaction."

—Douglas Conant, former Campbell Soup CEO and
author of *Touchpoints* and *The Blueprint*

Genuine career development is not about filling out forms, choreographing new assignments, or orchestrating promotions. It's about the quality of the conversations between a leader and an employee, conversations that are designed to

► Facilitate insights and awareness

► Explore possibilities and opportunities

► Inspire responses that drive employee-owned action

When it comes to the **leader's role** in development,

talk

is actually the most precious and results-driving commodity you have to share.

ONE AND DONE IS DONE

Responding to the ever-quickening pace of business, many organizations are rethinking a variety of time-honored (and time-consuming) practices. For instance, performance appraisals, once the centerpiece of management, are being eliminated or reconstituted in very different ways.

So what about career development? If you're like the vast majority of leaders expected to operate at the speed of business, you may no longer feel that you have the luxury of annual or semiannual development dialogues.

And that's not a problem—it's actually an opportunity. Because you don't have to hold lengthy summits with employees, solving all the career problems of the world in one big meeting to help others get results. In fact, in many cases less can be more.

After a few years, I realized what the annual development process reminded me of—New Year's resolutions! It was energizing to set out the plan, and we paid attention to it for a while. But pretty soon, it was tucked away until the following year when we'd smile at our folly and rededicate ourselves to a new batch.

—**Marketing director**

When you reframe *career development* in terms of ongoing conversations—rather than procedural checkpoints or scheduled activities—suddenly you have more flexibility and the chance to develop careers organically, when and where authentic opportunities arise.

LESS IS MORE

An interaction doesn't require a minimum time threshold to count as a conversation. You don't get more points for length. You get more points for stimulating thinking.

Would you rather ...

| Sit down with an employee for **2 hours** and map out a career plan for the year? | **or** | Do the same thing in a dozen **10-minute** conversations over the year? |

Note: Do the math. It's the same 120 minutes—just offered up in smaller, bite-size servings.

Increasingly, organizations and the time-starved leaders within them are opting for shorter, more frequent conversations that can cover the same ground as their heftier cousins—or maybe even more—but in an iterative and ongoing fashion. The benefits are compelling:

► Shorter conversations fit better with the cadence of business today.

► Frequent, ongoing dialogue communicates a genuine commitment to the employee and development.

► Iterative conversations allow employees to layer awareness, insights, and action more naturally.

► Treating development as a series of conversations acknowledges the reality that plans need to be agile and responsive to workplace changes.

► The ongoing nature of the conversation keeps development alive in everyone's mind (as opposed to tucking it away for a formal meeting), which can be particularly helpful when working with hybrid and remote employees.

► These frequent exchanges sustain momentum, fuel progress, and act as an ongoing reminder of the organization's commitment to employee learning, growth, and progress.

Some call it *embedded*. Others *on-the-fly, stealth,* or *in-the-moment.* We call it a contemporary solution to a perennial problem. Short, targeted, ongoing career conversations are efficient—for you and the employee—because they happen within the workflow where genuine opportunities exist.

BECOME UN^BALANCED

Think about the most interesting and engaging conversations you've experienced. Either you got to do most of the talking or the dialogue moved fluidly back and forth, allowing everyone to share airtime evenly. Now forget all that.

A career conversation is completely unbalanced in favor of your employees. If you do your job well, they will be doing 90 percent of the talking. If you're talking more than 10 percent of the time, you're likely taking on too much responsibility for employees' development and robbing them of ownership for their careers.

Striking this unbalance requires a particular skill on the part of the leader: asking quality questions.

> *My first real manager had this way of asking these questions that wormed their way into my brain and ultimately demanded answers.*
> —**Supervisor, finance and accounting**

If the work of career development happens within the context of conversation, the primary tool of the trade must be the question.

Thoughtfully conceived and well-timed questions make things happen. They

► Provoke reflection, constructive discomfort, insight, ideas, and action in others

► Keep the focus squarely on the employee

► Demonstrate that you respect and value the other person

► Reinforce the shift of ownership for development to the employee

You don't have to have all the **answers**.

But what's not negotiable is that you have the **questions**.

We are so sold on the value of questions that we've included 100 throughout this book.

PSYCHOLOGICAL SAFETY NET

Your organization may have given you *responsibility* for career development. But you've got to earn the *right* to ask the questions, facilitate an unbalanced conversation, and engage in the most intimate and meaningful parts of an employee's relationships with their work. Only employees can grant that right—and they grant it exclusively to those who cultivate a safe environment.

Psychological safety, a term introduced by Harvard professor and researcher Amy Edmondson, refers to feeling safe within the context of personal risk taking (and career development can feel pretty risky). It's about not feeling fear of punishment or humiliation for actions taken. And it's at the heart of a development relationship between leader and employee.

► Who's going to be open and honest in the assessment of their skills if they don't trust how the information they share will be used?

► Who's going to vulnerably request an opportunity if they think there may be negative consequences?

► Who's going to try to learn a new skill if they're afraid that failure could come with recriminations or worse?

Psychological safety is the key to getting a positive answer to any of these questions. It's an essential prerequisite for meaningful career dialogue and development. But it's not a mystical fog that settles over a relationship; it's built over time by leaders who, in addition to normalizing mistakes and instilling a growth mindset, also consistently demonstrate

► Benevolence—genuinely having the other person's best interest at heart

► Empathy—understanding, respecting, and honoring feelings, experiences, and different points of view

▶ Vulnerability—sharing weaknesses, struggles, and failures authentically

▶ Honesty—demonstrating integrity, openness, and transparency in word and deed

▶ Support—having the other person's back (especially when things veer off course)

Leaders who consistently demonstrate these behaviors weave the kind of psychological safety net that earns them the right to engage in the important and sometimes personal conversations at the heart of career development.

GROW YOUR CQ (CURIOSITY QUOTIENT)

Questions are a powerful tool. Add the spirit of curiosity, and you've got an unbeatable combination.

> **" I have no special talent.
> I am only passionately curious."**
>
> —Albert Einstein

But, let's face it—curiosity doesn't come quite as naturally or easily to many of us as adults as it did when we were kids. Blame it on time scarcity or information overload or our search-engine culture that reinforces a laser-like focus on what we think we want to know. Whatever is to blame, there's a powerful case for overcoming it, because curiosity is not just informative—it's also transformative.

People recognize and respond deeply to genuine curiosity on the part of their leaders. It leaves them feeling cared for, valued, and validated—all of which fuels stronger relationships, retention, and results.

Take the quiz on the next page to evaluate your level of curiosity.

WHAT ABOUT YOU?

Test your own Curiosity Quotient (CQ).

	Completely Disagree				Completely Agree
1. I am comfortable entering a conversation not knowing how it will turn out.	1	2	3	4	5
2. I can suspend judgment and skepticism.	1	2	3	4	5
3. I expect to be surprised when I talk with others.	1	2	3	4	5
4. I can suspend my need to fix situations and solve problems.	1	2	3	4	5
5. I am sincerely interested in what most people have to say.	1	2	3	4	5
6. I believe there's no shame in admitting I don't understand something.	1	2	3	4	5
7. I ask questions without having a "right" answer in mind.	1	2	3	4	5
8. I am energized by finding out what makes others tick.	1	2	3	4	5
9. I am motivated to dig deeper when I sense hesitancy or want to learn more.	1	2	3	4	5
10. I enjoy learning things about people that I didn't know before.	1	2	3	4	5
11. I am comfortable following someone else's lead in a conversation.	1	2	3	4	5
12. I believe that people are interesting and complex.	1	2	3	4	5

TOTAL: _____

If you scored 54 or higher, pat yourself on the back. You bring a remarkable amount of curiosity to your relationships and work. Keep up the good work.

Scores of 42 to 53 suggest that curiosity is a quality that's present in a lot of your interactions. Continue your good practices. Consider reviewing those items you rated lower, and get curious about how you might move them up a notch.

Scores of 41 or below might offer an opportunity for reflection on curiosity and the role it might play in relationships and your work. Identify the high-rated items and double down on continuing those. Consider identifying one or two of your lowest-rated items and discussing them with a friend or colleague.

Are you curious about how others view you? Download a digital assessment at help-them-grow.com/resources and invite your team to anonymously share their perspectives. While you understand your intentions around curiosity, they'll be able to share how those intentions are expressed and received through your behavior.

Curiosity might be the most under-the-radar and undervalued leadership competency in business today.

Think about it: What could you accomplish if you practiced passionate listening—really listening with intention and a true sense of purpose to learn and understand? What possibilities could you cultivate if you honed your ability to wonder out loud with those around you? What innovations and breakthroughs might you spark if you could bring new eyes and genuine inquisitiveness to old relationships and problems?

Developing the ability to approach individuals, situations, and conversations with curiosity can affect your own energy and enthusiasm, relationships with others, and hard business results—not to mention the quality of your career conversations.

You might be able to fake listening, but not curiosity.

HIGH-IMPACT PRACTICES

Four high-impact practices can help cultivate and bring greater curiosity to your interactions with others.

Lose control.

Curiosity is all about becoming comfortable with what's not known. Successful and curious managers know that this means consciously entering a conversation not knowing how it will turn out and asking questions you don't know the answers to. It means not guiding others toward the *right* answers you have in mind. It frequently means following someone else's conversational lead rather than your own. Curiosity means taking a leap of faith, letting go of the need to control, and trusting that all will unfold—perhaps even better than if you continue to force it.

Jettison judgment.

Be honest. How many words does someone speak before you've decided who they are, what they're like, or what they're trying to communicate? There's an epidemic of judgment and skepticism in the workplace. Perhaps it's because of time pressures. Perhaps it's due to confidence that our instincts will guide us. The reason matters less than this: curiosity and judgment cannot coexist. The most successful and curious leaders have developed the ability to suspend judgment. They engage fully without the need to put people or issues in tidy boxes. They appreciate the value of getting the whole story—especially when it comes to development.

GAG your "fix it" reflex.

You've risen to your management role because you're good at solving problems. Yet overused, this skill can endanger (and in some cases completely extinguish) curiosity. It's all too common for a leader to volunteer a resolution or generate elements of a development plan—all with the best of intentions. But engaging the other person promotes greater growth and allows leaders to learn more in the process.

WOO the cue.

Successful, curious leaders are not passive consumers of information. They engage actively with others. They are on high alert for signals and cues that require exploration. An emotionally charged word. A facial expression. A pause or hesitance. A reaction. All are invitations to dig deeper, follow up with thoughtful next-level questions, ask for examples, or just pause and invite the other person to say more. These cues are like traffic signs, helping leaders navigate the career conversation with curiosity and purpose.

Quality questions		Quality questions
asked mechanically *without* curiosity will signal to employees that you're going through the motions or have just come back from training.	**but**	asked *with* the spirit of curiosity will facilitate conversations that will allow others to literally change their lives.

CLOSURE IS OVERRATED

Given this focus on asking questions, we can't say it enough: you don't have to have all the answers. Neither does the employee. In fact, not having all the answers may actually drive more thought and energy.

According to Russian psychologist Bluma Zeigarnik (in "The Retention of Completed and Uncompleted Actions," which appeared in *Psychological Research* in 1927), people remember better what's incomplete. For many people, this lack of closure generates an internal tension. The mind, uncomfortable with what has been left unfinished, continues to focus on the question or problem.

So what does this science have to do with helping your people grow? Many leaders shy away from hard questions and conversations where they or others might not have all the answers. If you're one of them, stop! Go ahead and courageously ask the challenging questions and even conclude a conversation with a real tough or thought-provoking one. Then

Closure is overrated.

Unfinished business causes employees to **continue pondering**…

and who knows what will happen from there.

invite the employee to noodle for a while. The lack of closure itself may lead to deeper thinking and richer conversations. (They'll appreciate the opportunity to reflect and reconnect with you when they're ready.)

Don't feel the pressure to wrap up every conversation with a bow.

► TRY THIS: AN OPEN-ENDED QUESTION
- -

End your next meeting or conversation with a question. Explain that there's no time for a discussion, but that you've been thinking about the issue. The next time you are with that person or those people, ask if anyone remembers the question. You'll be surprised that not only do they remember the question, they'll likely also have quite a few answers for you.

HINDSIGHT, FORESIGHT, INSIGHT

So what are all these unbalanced, psychologically safe, curious, unfinished conversations supposed to be about? More than you might expect. Too frequently we limit the scope of career conversations, think-

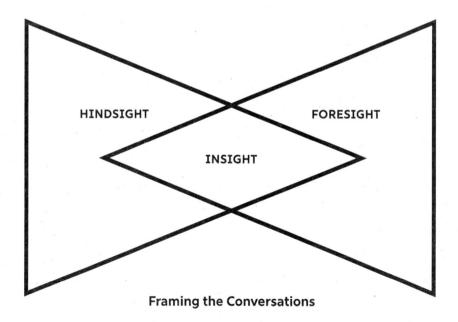

Framing the Conversations

ing they're only about jobs, promotions, or stretch assignments—the actions employees can take to move forward. Important? Yes. But that's just a drop in the bucket of conversations you can have with employees.

Whether your conversations are more formal and lengthy or shorter and iterative, helping others pursue their career goals involves facilitating an exploration of three key areas: hindsight, foresight, and insight.

Hindsight. This is a look backward to develop a deep understanding of such things as where employees have been, what they love, and what they're good at. Self-perception is key, and it becomes even clearer when enhanced (and sometimes moderated) by feedback gathered from others. This backward glance—on the part of the employee and those around them—is essential for moving forward.

Foresight. This involves a bigger-picture look at the broader environment and the business in order to determine what's changing and what those changes mean for the future. Since nobody wants to pursue a career direction for which no need exists, foresight is critical.

Insight. This is the sweet spot where hindsight (where you've been and what you want to be doing) converges with foresight (organizational needs and opportunities). It's where you and the employee jointly determine the full range of ways to move forward and the actions to take to achieve career objectives.

This is not an academic model cooked up in a social science lab. It's a framework (based on more than fifty years of working with real people and their real challenges) that flexes to address the many types of career conversations available to leaders. This framework operates and supports you on three levels:

Micro — You can ask a question from any of the three areas to informally spark reflection and interest.

Macro — You can blend the three areas into one short conversation that can occur spontaneously in the workflow to help employees advance their career thinking.

Mega — You can apply this framework and the questions associated with hindsight, foresight, and insight to your organization's formal individual development planning (IDP) process for richer results.

The following chapters delve into hindsight, foresight, and insight and how you can use them to keep employees satisfied, engaged, and always growing.

What IF . . .

► your job was to facilitate conversations rich with insightful questions that would guide others toward greater awareness and action?

► you got just a little bit more curious?

► you didn't pressure yourself to have all the answers?

Let **HINDSIGHT** Light the Way

My interview for this job was so great. The manager was really interested in learning about my background and how I'd applied myself in the past. He asked great, probing questions that really challenged me to think. I sure wish he would "interview" me like that again now that I've got the job.

—An employee (perhaps yours)

Imagine if the job interview was the beginning of an ongoing conversational thread throughout someone's career. Imagine uncovering layer upon layer of your employees' skills, abilities, interests, and more—right up to the day they retire. Imagine what you could do with that information. Imagine what the employee could do with it.

LOOKING BACK TO MOVE FORWARD

You can enable career-advancing self-awareness by helping employees take stock of where they've been, what they've done, and who they are. Looking back thoughtfully is what hindsight conversations are all about. They surface what people need to know and understand about themselves to approach future career steps in a productive and satisfying way.

"You can't connect the dots looking forward; you can only connect them looking backwards."

—Steve Jobs, cofounder, Apple

For hindsight to be as clear as possible, though, two different perspectives are required. The employee's self-perception is the starting point. (That's what this chapter is all about.) But it needs to be confirmed, challenged, enhanced, and otherwise worked over with information gathered from others. When employees, coworkers, and you (the manager) also look back at performance and results, hindsight gets that much closer to 20/20. (Just wait until the next chapter for more about feedback.)

Hindsight allows employees to develop a clear view of their

► Skills and strengths—what they're good at

► Values—what's most important and creates a sense of meaning

► Interests—what keeps them engaged

► Dislikes—what they want to steer clear of

► Preferences—how they like to work

► Weaknesses—what they struggle with

Clarity around these factors allows for intentional movement toward career objectives. Otherwise, people may engage in lots of activity that's not focused or that takes them in directions that aren't consistent with who they are and what they really want to do.

> *I worked for years to get that senior troubleshooter promotion. Put everything into it. But when I got it, I was miserable. The travel was really unsatisfying. I'd swoop in, do my part, and then swoop out— never seeing the end product or really feeling a part of it. If I'd really thought about it, I would have known that it wasn't a good fit. I've always been happiest being part of an ongoing team and having something tangible to show for my efforts at the end of the day.*
>
> —IT consultant

Your organization may have access to or actively use assessments and systems like StrengthFinder or DISC. By all means, use them. They offer employees greater self-awareness and offer you a window to the individual. They can generate exceptional fodder for informing hindsight.

Your employees' ability to take satisfying and productive steps toward

career goals

is directly proportionate to their **self-awareness.**

But it's the hindsight conversations that are at the heart of career development. Using all available inputs, they are designed to spark thinking, encourage connections, and promote discovery. They provide invaluable information to the employee and to you, the leader. You can facilitate this type of self-awareness through quality questions that

► Haunt the employee, popping out around every corner

► Percolate throughout the day—and maybe at night

► Worm their way around employees' minds, encouraging new areas to explore

Employees may get "**there**" only to discover that it's not really where they wanted to be.

If you're still waiting for the other shoe to drop and for us to tell you about the ten to twenty hours of additional to-dos that are required to appropriately support your employees in their career development, let it go. It's not going to happen. You can be highly effective by just guiding the conversation. You don't have to have the answers, and you don't have to drive the action.

THE GRAVITATIONAL PULL OF WEAKNESSES

Despite considerable research and literature on the benefits of focusing on strengths, most people are more strongly drawn toward and familiar with their weaknesses. When you have a minute—literally sixty seconds—make a list of all of your strengths and weaknesses. Chances are you'll have more weaknesses than strengths on your list.

In fact, in workshop after workshop we witness a surprising human dynamic. When people are asked to create a list of their weaknesses, they do so effortlessly, smiling and sometimes laughing at the task. Ask these same people to list their strengths, and you see a very different response. Furrowed brows. Head scratching. Grimaces and genuine agitation. Odd, huh?

WHAT ABOUT YOU?

You can even skip the writing and count your strengths on one hand and weaknesses on the other. More smiles or frowns?

Employees need your help in identifying and focusing on what they do well—their talents and their gifts. These are important inputs to career decisions that frequently get lost in our weakness-centric world.

But strengths can be a little sneaky—and employees should be aware of two lesser-known laws that govern them.

Law 1—Too much of a good thing isn't always a good thing. A strength used to excess can actually become a problem and hurt effectiveness.

When it's just right	When it's overdone
"He's organized and meets deadlines no matter what."	"You mean old steamroller?"
"Her flexible thinking really helps everyone get outside the box."	"Our weekly meetings are a total waste of time because of her lack of structure."
"He's a great negotiator."	"It wouldn't hurt him to compromise once in a while."

Strengths have a dark side. Getting in touch with the implications of too-much-of-a-good-thing helps to enhance one's self-understanding—and ultimately effectiveness.

Law 2—Strengths are context sensitive. A strength in one setting can actually work against you in other settings. (Remember when you were first promoted into leadership? Did your strength around getting the work done ever get in the way of delegating or developing others?)

With all this talk of strengths, let's not lose sight of the importance of understanding weaknesses, where behavior or performance could compromise an employee's career goals. Because when it comes to helping people grow and pursue career goals, a balanced view of what's working for and against you provides the strongest foundation for results.

A **strength** is a lot like **oxygen.**

We don't pay much attention to it— unless it's **missing.**

Hindsight conversations don't need to be long or take a lot of planning time. Here are three "Try This" activities that you can prepare for in two minutes and conduct in as little as five- to ten-minute chunks around the other work that needs to get done. Choose any or all depending upon your level of comfort and the nature of the relationship and level of trust you've established with your employees.

► TRY THIS: GET TO KNOW THEM BACKWARD
- -

Schedule a conversation to deliberately review an employee's past experiences, jobs, positions, and tasks to find themes, trends, and insights.

1. Start by explaining that a solid career future is based upon an understanding of who you are and what got you to where you are.

2. With the employee, create a list of the various positions, roles, and jobs they have held.

3. For each position, role, or job, ask the following questions:

   ► Which parts brought you joy, energy, and a sense of persistence?

   ► Which parts led to boredom, disengagement, and a sense of just going through the motions?

4. Step back with the employee and see what themes emerge. You won't need a PhD or psychoanalysis couch to make connections. Using questions like these will help:

   ► What thoughts and ideas came up repeatedly?

   ► How might your interests, values, and skills have evolved over time?

   ► What will you definitely want to seek out in the future?

   ► What will you definitely want to avoid in the future?

It's that straightforward. You ask the questions. They answer. And together you make sense out of it.

► TRY THIS: QUARTERLY CHECKUP

A variation of the Get-to-Know-Them-Backward theme is to close out every quarter with brief employee checkups or check-ins. The purpose of these conversations is not to evaluate business results, review sales, or negotiate productivity standards for the next quarter. Rather, the goal is to diagnose what's going on in the employee's heart and head.

Put performance entirely aside and ask questions like these:

- ► What was the best part of the quarter for you?
- ► What work did you find most satisfying?
- ► How often were you stretched, and how did that feel?
- ► At what points did you feel your energy and engagement lagging?

Make this a habit, and at least four times each year you'll help employees turn their day-to-day experiences into profound self-awareness that can inform career decisions—and a lot more.

► TRY THIS: THE NEVER-ENDING INTERVIEW

Keep the interview going by engaging in routine conversations that reveal an ever-evolving, complex, and multidimensional picture to the employee of what will be important to consider as a basis for career growth.

5. Just pull one or more questions that most interest you and the employee from the list that follows. Use them in any order. Take notes.

Skills and Strengths

- ► What have you always been naturally good at?
- ► What can't you keep yourself from doing?
- ► What are you known for?

Values

► Looking back, what's always been most important to you in life and in work?

► What issues or problems do you feel most strongly about?

► What are your top three values or things you hold most dear?

Interests

► What do you enjoy learning about most?

► What do you wish you had more time for?

► How would you spend your time if you didn't have to work?

Dislikes

► What kind of work have you typically gravitated away from?

► What tasks routinely get pushed to the bottom of your to-do list?

► What bores you?

Preferences

► What aspects of past jobs have you loved most?

► How do you like to work?

► What kinds of work settings or spaces help you do your best work?

Weaknesses/Opportunities

► What lessons do you find yourself learning over and over again?

► How do your strengths sometimes work against you?

► What skills do you appreciate in others that you don't always see in yourself?

6. Together determine what conclusions can be drawn by asking questions such as these:

- ► How do these pieces fall together?

- ► What picture or image do they yield?

- ► What are the commonalities, themes, or connection points?

Skills, strengths, values, interests, dislikes, preferences, and weaknesses converge in unique ways for each individual—like snowflakes or fingerprints. As understanding about these things grows, people start to see an image appear that becomes a clearer picture of their lives and who they are.

But this awareness cannot be contained to career matters. Greater personal insight can't help but spill over into day-to-day work, improving relationships, performance, and results. It starts to seep into one's personal life, enhancing that as well. Hindsight conversations are good for the whole person—not just for the part people bring to work.

Don't be fooled. These approaches are simple, straightforward, and relatively quick. But they pack a punch. In fact, they deliver value far beyond their modest appearances.

CASE IN POINT

I was born to teach. It was pretty obvious from the way I was frequently the first to figure out new processes and applications and teach them to the rest of the group. My earliest memory was of getting in trouble when I (proudly) taught a fellow kindergartner how to write the first letter of her name—on the carpet. Over the years, I've found my greatest satisfaction to be in roles where I connect with and help others learn and grow. I really appreciate my manager recognizing that and encouraging me to explore opportunities in training.

—Technical trainer

It's easy to pigeonhole people. Figure out what they're good at and forget the rest. Take Pat, the rock star we hired away from a competitor to manage our challenging clients. She seemed happy doing what she was doing. Once or twice we upgraded her title. All of a sudden, she resigned to take a sales job. It turns out that she had felt bored for years—was tired of what she was doing. If it had occurred to me to look past the one skill set that we myopically capitalized on, she'd still be with us today—bringing in much-needed new business.

—Director, commercial lines insurance

COUNTERPOINT

Fundamentally people want to know themselves and be known by others. Hindsight conversations satisfy that deep human need.

But helping people look back and inward also provides a reservoir of information that allows employees to move forward and toward their career goals in intentional ways that will produce satisfying results.

Anytime is a great time for a hindsight conversation.

What IF...

► a little time was spent looking back before leaping forward?

► managers had the questions to help unlock what's unique within and important to each employee?

► you applied the curiosity you bring to first interviews to ongoing conversations with employees throughout their careers?

FEED
Me

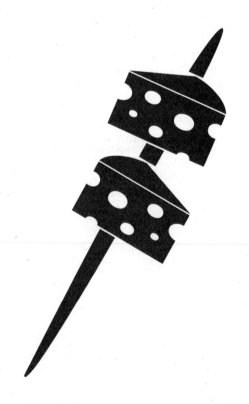

Where do I stand? How am I seen? What do you think? I don't mean to sound needy—but since I'm no longer in the office with my manager and team every day, I just don't know.

—An employee (perhaps yours)

Feedback. How appropriate that the word begins with *feed*. For many employees, lack of information from others about how they're perceived and how they're doing is a severe source of malnourishment in today's workplace.

In study after study, data suggests that employees are starving for feedback. This is a pretty human response. We spend more than forty hours each week at work, dedicating our bodies, minds, and souls to the cause. A little attention is not too much to ask.

Leaders, beware: a low-feedback diet may be harmful to the health of your business. Side effects include

- Disengagement
- Lost opportunities
- Stunted growth
- Lack of clarity
- Loss of talent

Good people move on—either psychologically or physically—when their hunger for feedback isn't satisfied. And this loss of talent is completely unnecessary because feedback

- Costs nothing except a little genuine attention to others
- Lends itself to literally any setting—face-to-face or virtual
- Requires as little as a minute of your time
- Extends far beyond the domain of leaders—anyone who is willing or asked can get involved

Feedback is a hindsight lens through which people can pass their self-perceptions—and in the process, it yields a clearer vision of who they are and the value they bring. Effective feedback planted in a receptive mind can fuel powerful learning, exploration, challenge, and growth.

WHAT ABOUT YOU?

Be honest. When it comes to giving and getting feedback, where do you stand?

May I please make an appointment for a root canal?								No dessert for me, I'll have feedback instead!

1   **10**

While root canals over dessert might be an exaggeration, let's face it: the average leader isn't likely to list feedback as one of the best parts of their job. For many, it's anxiety producing. They fear all that might go wrong—wrong timing, wrong example, wrong tone. Will I hurt their feelings? Will it hurt their productivity? Will it hurt our relationship? These are all fair concerns.

But what's frequently forgotten is all that can go right—even when feedback is delivered clumsily or imperfectly. A stronger connection. Better understanding. Greater trust. Clearer focus. Heightened motivation. So don't schedule that root canal just yet; you might be ordering feedback for dessert by the end of the chapter.

IT'S FEEDING TIME

Opportunities for feedback abound. What probably comes to your mind first is performance feedback—job-related information about an employee's behavior or results that helps to drive improvement. That's important—but it's a small subset of what we're talking about here. We're talking about a broader and more expansive dialogue that drives development.

We've just discussed the value of hindsight conversations, which surface essential information from the employee's point of view. The problem is that the individual's perspective is rarely a complete picture. The employee needs a reality check—an opportunity to expand their perspective beyond their own point of view and round out their self-assessment. Voilà! An opportunity for feedback.

Helping employees proactively solicit the perceptions of others offers them many benefits:

► They're able to check their assumptions, expand their understanding of themselves, and discover who they are in the eyes of others.

► They develop the capacity to independently initiate feedback conversations.

► They build stronger, more collaborative, and trust-based relationships.

Do this well enough for long enough, and pretty soon you'll have a self-generating feeding frenzy—in a good way—in which employees become comfortable volunteering and receiving feedback freely among themselves.

WHO'S WHO IN THEIR ZOO

Feedback is another sort of a hindsight conversation. The good, the bad, and the ugly are confirmed or dispelled as the employee's perspective is checked against the points of view held by others.

To ensure the most complete picture, it's important to tap into the broadest career audience possible. Ask employees who in their lives—both inside and outside the organization—might have insights into them and their strengths, abilities, interests, and opportunities. The answer will likely include some combination of

- ► Peers
- ► Employees
- ► Contractors

- ► Interns
- ► Customers
- ► Suppliers

- ► Family
- ► Friends
- ► Leader

You'll notice that you—the leader—are last on the list. And that's to make an important point.

When it comes to career development, it takes a **village.**

As the leader, you have a unique perspective. But yours is one of many that will inform the employee's understanding of themselves and help be the basis for effective development and planning.

Employees need to develop the broadest network possible to facilitate their career success. Coworkers and others within and outside the organization have potentially important information, ideas, and helpful contacts. And gathering feedback from them is an ideal way for employees to begin to take ownership for their careers and engage others in creating and supporting their paths forward.

So encourage employees to gather feedback from others before sharing your own. It's not about politeness (e.g., letting the guests get their food first); it's about power. You've got it, and as a result your perspective may carry undue weight. When employees come to you with a plate full of feedback from others, they are better able to put your perspective into perspective.

JUST REMEMBER: **ABC**

Soliciting and accepting feedback graciously are skills that distinguish successful and effective individuals. Yet many people have not had the benefit of learning these skills. Your employees are likely among them.

Since the act of opening oneself up to the opinions of others can be challenging, the agenda for such a discussion should be simple—as straightforward as ABC. Encourage employees to focus on just three things as they gather feedback from others: abilities, blind spots, and conditions.

Abilities

► What are my greatest strengths?

► Which of my skills are most valuable?

► What can you always count on me for?

► What value do I bring?

Blind Spots

► What behaviors have you observed that might get in my way?

► How have I fallen short of expectations?

► How might my strengths work against me?

► What one change could I make that would have the greatest positive effect on my success?

Conditions

► In what settings or under what circumstances do I make the greatest contributions?

► Under what conditions have you observed me struggling?

► Do I tend to perform best when working with others or flying solo?

► What factors have you noticed trigger stress or other negative reactions for me?

These specific, concrete questions demand specific, concrete responses. They generate considerably more actionable information than the lazy feedback default question "How am I doing?"—which normally generates a tepid thumbs up.

So work with employees to select a question or two from each category to use as the starting point for feedback conversations with individuals in their career networks.

Then, be prepared to debrief these conversations. At first, people might need help overcoming the natural human response to focus on the data that validates their existing world view. They may need help evaluating (rather than arguing with or defending against) multiple perspectives to recognize and identify common threads and themes. They may need help making sense of seemingly contradictory information. Investing time with others to process feedback sends a strong message to employees and provides you with additional information to support that person's growth.

As you can imagine, live, face-to-face feedback conversations are ideal. But, given today's distributed workforce, employees may need to resort to virtual means. Whatever form it takes, this sort of real-time interaction can surface valuable information while strengthening relationships.

Greater awareness and stronger relationships support career development. In this way, feedback really does help employees grow where they are, so they won't go and grow somewhere else. As a bonus, they develop a critical skill that leads to greater success on the job and in life. And if you have an online tool that you love, keep using it—in addition to, not *instead of*, conversation.

CHECK YOUR INTENTIONS

You might have been at the end of that list of those who provide feedback, but you're not forgotten. You are a critical part of your employees' career audience too, which means that they'll be looking to you to share your perspective as well as your opinions about their abilities, blind spots, and the conditions that support their success. Your role is to be your employees' honest advocate, someone they can count on for candor but also for support.

> *I can hear almost anything she has to say because I know deep down that she's on my side.*
>
> —Registered nurse

But before you earn the right to offer feedback that others will take to heart, it's essential to do an intention check. The verbal formula you follow when delivering feedback matters less than the intentions you bring to the conversation.

The **motivation** of the feedback-giver trumps technique.

The **spirit** of the message overrides its syntax.

What comes from the **heart** overshadows what comes out of our mouths.

When getting ready to offer feedback, ask yourself, *What's my intention?* If it's to get something off your chest or make someone else wrong, you might want to think twice. Your intentions speak considerably louder than the words you choose. So make sure that all feedback is rooted in a sincere desire to be of service to someone's growth.

When you marry a positive intent with well-chosen words, you create an unbeatable platform for helping others absorb, understand, and take action based on your feedback.

FRAME YOUR FEEDBACK

Organizing your thoughts and words for optimal impact can be as easy as following these three steps:

1. **Focus on the WHAT.** The *what* refers to the specific, concrete behaviors and results that have a bearing on the employee's career direction and progression. Be as specific as you can, sharing the details necessary to ensure a complete understanding. But don't stop there.

2. **Follow up with SO WHAT.** Explore the impact of the behavior and results you highlight. This provides a context for your feedback and helps the employee make sense of your feedback in terms of career development and direction.

   ▶ **Don't say:** You're a great rep. Keep up the good work.

   ▶ **Do say:** You consistently offer creative solutions to our customers' problems. Your behavior is the standard that new reps see and emulate. You're becoming a real leader of the team.

3. **Explore the NOW WHAT.** Feedback—whether positive or negative—offers an opportunity for reflection and possible action. If the feedback validates what the employee is currently doing, it's a chance to consider how to build upon success or leverage strengths in new ways. If the feedback suggests opportunities for improvement, it's a chance to make different choices or learn new skills and approaches. In either case, the key is for you to ask insightful questions like

- ► What's your reaction to this?

- ► What does this mean to you?

- ► What do you want to do with this information?

- ► What steps might you consider taking?

- ► What's in it for you to take these steps or make these changes?

- ► Whose help might you recruit?

- ► What support do you need?

This simple framework—when combined with your positive intention—offers a multipurpose roadmap that supports career conversations, performance feedback, and even clear, actionable communication outside of the workplace.

USE CANDOR AND CARE

There is no either/or choice between candor and care. It's both/and. Employees care deeply about what their leaders feel and think about them. And their ability to hear a tough message is directly proportionate to the care with which you deliver it. The few minutes you take to consider and frame your feedback can make a tremendous difference in terms of its reception and usefulness.

- ► **Don't say:** You just don't seem to be able to cut it in sales.

- ► **Do say:** You have the ability to develop strong relationships with customers. Those relationships, though, aren't translating into sales. Let's talk about how we can better use your skills and strengths.

Brain researchers find that people experience the same physiological responses to feedback as they do to physical threats. (You probably could have told them that based on how the mere mention of "feedback" makes your heart pound a bit faster and makes the moisture in your mouth suddenly find its way to your brow.) Leading with strengths, talents, and skills can create greater psychological safety and help others remain more present and receptive to the more sensitive information you have to share.

❝Most people want to hear the truth, even if it is unpalatable—there is something within us that responds deeply to people who level with us.❞

—Susan Scott, author of *Fierce Conversations*

WHAT ABOUT YOU? -

How frequently do you seek out feedback from others? How receptive are you to information about your performance or behavior?

How gracious and appreciative are you when someone points out something you could do better? You set the tone for your team.
A feedback-rich culture begins with you. Do you want a free flow of feedback? Start modeling what it looks like to solicit, welcome, and use feedback from others.

A FEEDBACK FOCUS

Don't know where to start? Or do you want to expand your feedback focus to better support your employees' growth? Look no further. Employees need to get information from you around three key areas: technical skills, soft skills, and today's non-negotiables.

Technical or hard skills are those that relate specifically to how employees produce the outputs of their jobs. Whether it's welding or website design, selling or shift management, hard skills are the fundamentals of performing one's work—and what we typically think of first when we consider what's needed to be successful in a role and beyond. But that's just the tip of the iceberg. What's equally important (more important according to some) is the set of interpersonal competencies that enable someone's success. This includes things like communication, collaboration, teamwork, and networking. And anyone who's ever struggled to master them knows that these soft skills can be pretty hard.

There's yet another category that's frequently forgotten, operating below the surface as a set of meta-competencies that are today's non-negotiables. Given the pace, pressure, uncertainty, and complexity that characterize the modern workplace, success demands a commitment to

► Self-awareness—In a world where reflection is quickly becoming a lost art, those who take the time to look inward, make sense of their motivations and actions, and learn from their experiences and strengths build a solid base of personal understanding from which to operate more effectively, ethically, and with greater authenticity.

► Passionate curiosity—An enduring sense of wonder about the world and the possibilities it holds helps people not just befriend but partner with uncertainty and change in a way that makes it work for them.

► Continuous and anticipatory learning—Regardless of the field or discipline, the only constant we can count on is change. That's why employees who proactively and regularly seek out new information and skills—even before they're needed—set themselves up to thrive.

► Real-time resilience—There's no shortage of problems, issues, or disappointments in today's workplace. Setbacks are a given—and frequently evidence that someone is engaged in a productive challenge. The key to sustainable success (and reduced stress) is implementing strategies to maintain a positive attitude, effectively and quickly bounce back, and keep moving forward.

While people may be hardwired with a greater or lesser tendency toward these non-negotiables, they are skills that can definitely be developed over time—and with your supportive feedback.

Address any of these areas—technical skills, soft skills, or today's non-negotiables—and you'll plant important developmental seeds. Combine a couple for a powerful and enlightening conversation. Add them all to your list of possible feedback topics to address over time as you share your perspective in support of your employees' growth.

What IF...

▶ everyone enjoyed clarity about who they are, what they're good at, where opportunities to improve exist, and where they could make the greatest difference?

▶ employees felt comfortable asking for and receiving feedback?

▶ leaders were not the only ones empowered and able to provide feedback?

— 5 —

What's
HAPPENING?

Telling me that the business landscape is changing is like telling a polar bear it's cold outside. I know. I live it. But there's got to be a better way than always scrambling and reacting. I don't want to just keep up—I want to get ahead of the curve.

—An employee (perhaps yours)

We are not going to tell you the world is changing. You could write that book. The changes and challenges you face every day frame your decisions about strategy, resource allocation, and other critical business matters.

Shouldn't they frame career decisions as well? (Answer: a resounding yes.)

Hindsight conversations provide a solid grounding in who the full person really is and what they bring to the party. But pursuing career growth with this clarity alone is a dangerous proposition. It can send people in directions that are interesting and may play to their strengths—but it might not necessarily serve a business need.

Hindsight clarity must be filtered through the lens of foresight—especially given the pace, scope, and magnitude of change. Foresight conversations open people's minds to the broader world, the future, organizational issues, changes, and the implications of all of these. In this way, foresight helps people focus their career efforts in ways that will lead to satisfying and productive outcomes. It also provides context and perspective that enhance people's day-to-day work.

BEYOND THE CRYSTAL BALL

Stories of (and fear related to) skills stagnation and the full-blown extinction of formerly vital roles abound. But there are just as many stories of those who anticipated the future and were ready to grow into

Some people have an innate ability to keep their **eyes open** to the world around them.

To spot **trends** where others see unconnected dots.

To play out the **implications** of a seemingly insignificant event.

it. These aren't just high-profile business legends, but also mere mortals who work on the ground floor and seem to have the gift of living just a little further out in the future than the rest of us.

These people are probably not psychics. But they do practice their own brand of ESP: **Ever Scanning and Pondering.**

While it may come naturally to some, you can nurture it in others. ESP is a set of habits—habits that you can help employees build through ongoing foresight conversations.

FOSTERING FORESIGHT

You've been to the meetings (or not) and read the memos (or not). You know the big picture for your organization (or not). You may lay awake at night worrying about it, or you've so internalized it that it's always operating under the surface, unconsciously informing much of what you do. But many employees aren't making the connection between this big-picture information and its profound ramifications for the organization and themselves.

> **"You cannot listen for the future if you are deafened by the present or stuck in the past."**
>
> —Bob Johansen, author of *The New Leadership Literacies: Thriving in a Future of Extreme Disruption and Distributed Everything*

So populate their radar screens with a constellation of new points to consider

- ► External challenges and changes—what's going on in the world, including changing demographics, globalization, competition, government regulation, geopolitical forces, and economic shifts

- ► Internal challenges and changes—what's going on within the organization, including changing customer expectations, new vendor relationships, mergers and acquisitions, the evolving employment landscape, and responses to shrinking margins

*Don't seat me at the kids' table. I might not be an executive, but I
know there are changes coming. Let me in on things. I deserve to
know, whether I can do anything about it or not.*

—Production worker

Don't worry—we're not suggesting that you deliver a whole strategic
planning curriculum to your staff. On the contrary, we're just suggesting that you create a forum for employees to get in touch with the world
around them—the world that defines their career development playing
fields.

▶ TRY THIS: HARNESS MORE HEADS
- -

Whereas most career conversations are personal, one-on-one interactions
between the employee and leader, foresight conversations lend themselves
to a group context, making this not just a collaborative but also a highly efficient approach to development.

Get your team gathering information, researching issues, and having
direct experiences that deliver a visceral understanding of business changes
and challenges. Intellectual understanding is one thing. But hearing a customer's pain first-hand, seeing with their own eyes how products and services work (or don't), listening in on stakeholder or investor calls—that drives
the message far deeper and helps employees internalize the reality that's
shaping the world, your organization, and their careers.

Nobody can be an expert on all of the forces and factors shaping the
world, business, or your organization—not even you. So let the wisdom of
your crowd take over. Two, three, four, or more heads are better than one.
Encourage activities and conversations that will help all employees develop
the ESP habit.

Here's a starter list of ways people can begin to develop a visceral understanding of what's happening in the world around them. But between you and your employees, you'll likely come up with plenty more.

- ► Interview key individuals

- ► Engage in focused customer contact

- ► Research important issues or trends

- ► Read trade publications

- ► Participate in industry conferences

- ► Attend management or other cross-functional meetings

These activities will spark awareness and insight about the bigger picture—that is, what's going on in the world, the industry, and the organization itself. But the conversation and ensuing reflection can translate insight into a deep and useful understanding of the issues and their implications.

Simple questions that help people connect the dots go a long way:

- ► What are some of the most important things you learned?

- ► What might these things mean to our industry?

- ► What might they mean to our organization?

- ► How might they affect our products, services, or revenue stream?

- ► How might they impact our department?

- ► What do they mean for you, your job, and your career goals?

FORESIGHT FORUMS

Really want to make a difference? Consider institutionalizing foresight conversations by putting them on every meeting agenda. Have employees report on what they've learned. Explore what's changing. Hold an open discussion using the questions listed earlier.

Give employees a **visceral, first-hand** foresight experience by allowing them to **interact directly** with the changing business environment.

I started asking different staff members to kick off our meetings with a brief headline review—something from a trade publication, business journal, or general news. They gave a two-minute overview of the article and led a brief discussion about what it meant to us. I was surprised by the insights the group generated and how engaged they became. One week I forgot to include it on the agenda—and they let me know about it.

—Risk manager

Imagine what could happen if you started each staff meeting with a focus on foresight. The results would be powerful. Every employee would develop greater clarity that would help to inform career development and decisions.

But you'll soon discover that this is only part of the benefits of group foresight conversations. You'll learn more than you might expect. Employees will begin acting like business partners. You may even see more innovation and better results. Who knows what you'll accomplish... world peace? (That last one was just to make sure you were paying attention.)

► TRY THIS: FILL IN THE BLANKS
- -

Another approach to engaging employees in big-picture conversations is to set aside a few minutes and ask them to complete provocative sentence stems, such as

► The most significant change I've seen in our industry is

_____

► I predict that the next big thing will be

_____

► I can imagine a time when

_____

► Our business would be turned upside down if

_____

► Everything will change with the obsolescence of

_____

► I was most personally affected when the organization changed

_____

► It really made a difference when management

_____

► To keep my edge and pursue my career goals, I'm going to need to

_____

Pick one or more. Do it individually. Or do it with the team as a whole. And watch the conversation unfold.

Don't be fooled. These sentence stems are as powerful as they are simple. They force employees—sometimes for the first time—to step back and think more broadly and strategically about the world around them and what it means for their careers.

WHAT ABOUT YOU?

Consider these sentence stems yourself. How would you complete them? What do your responses mean in terms of what you'd like to be doing with your career?

DISRUPT OR BE DISRUPTED

We don't need to tell you that products and services that are viable today can become obsolete tomorrow. In response to this challenging and unpredictable reality, most organizations include innovation as a key strategic objective. But mere incrementalism may not be sufficient to survive and thrive. Disruption or radical change is the new normal. Organizations can certainly choose not to proactively disrupt, but in that case they'd better prepare to be disrupted themselves.

Even the employment landscape reflects this disruptive dynamic. The workplace of the past was completely populated with full-time employees. Today, it's a patchwork quilt of badge types and employment forms—full-time, part-time, contractor, consultant, intern, extern... and the list goes on. Where, when, and how people work is in flux.

Individual responses to all of this disruption depend in large part upon our point of view. Is the glass half scary or half exciting? Disruption brings with it new challenges, accelerated learning, and sustainable engagement. Particularly as employees live and work longer, disruption offers the opportunity to retain your people by keeping them interested and growing right where they are.

> **" When you disrupt yourself, you step back from who you are to slingshot into who you want to be."**
> —Whitney Johnson, author of *Disrupt Yourself*

Embracing disruption and the massive opportunities that come with it requires employees to be ready, receptive, and resilient. Whether someone comes out feeling vulnerable or victorious depends largely upon one thing: their level of agility.

THE AGILE ADVANTAGE

At its core, agility is all about staying current, keeping pace, shifting gears, responding fluidly—and doing it all nimbly and quickly. It's about preparing oneself to remain in a perpetual state of readiness to perceive and pivot toward possibilities.

Agility is the **secret sauce** of sustainable success.

While *foresight* offers an understanding of what's happening within the bigger picture and why, *agility* offers the ability to leverage that understanding—to make it work in your favor by taking smart and responsive actions. And you'll notice we use the word *actions* here—in its plural form. Given the dynamic and disruptive nature of today's workplace, singular paths forward must give way to multiple concurrent strategies and steps. This approach mitigates risk and offers the flexibility required to navigate quickly shifting conditions—because when it comes to business and careers, everyone needs to keep their options open. Agility lets you leverage foresight, translating it into smart, responsive steps forward.

So hindsight is powerful but incomplete without the overlay of foresight. What's happening in the changing world around us plays directly into career decisions, strategies, and success. Agile employees can make the disruptions and changes work for them with the help of some new habits—habits built and instilled through foresight conversations.

The intersection between hindsight and foresight is insight.

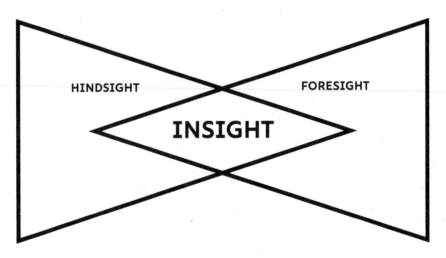

HINDSIGHT   FORESIGHT

INSIGHT

And the possible insights are endless:

► A new skill might be deployed to solve a problem.

► Evolving interests might support a new business direction.

► A long-held goal might be pursued through a vital project.

Insights that are recognized, explored, and exploited through career conversations with employees could uncover countless possibilities that will help them grow.

What IF...

► employees could develop the habit of scanning and pondering the environment around them?

► foresight conversations were a part of day-to-day life in your organization?

► disruption was welcomed as an opportunity for individual and organizational growth?

If Not Up,

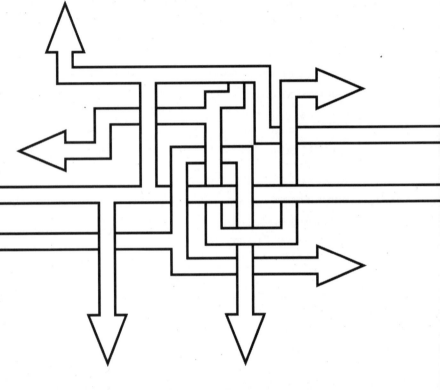

THEN WHAT?

Challenge me. Stretch me. I'm not as worried about being promoted as I am about learning, growing, and seeing my talents used in new and different ways.

—An employee (perhaps yours)

Insight and growth are all about possibilities. The problem is that managers and employees alike frequently have an outdated view of what those possibilities are. Growth in today's business environment means bidding adieu to some old thinking.

Say goodbye to the career ladder. Organizational belt-tightening and delayering continue to eat away at the leadership headcount in most organizations. The upper layers of the pyramid (which have always been slimmer) have become a mere sliver.

Say goodbye to limiting career paths. The predictable progression from one established position to the next has given way to career patterns. These are more fluid, flexible, and responsive to the needs of the business and the individual.

Say goodbye to checking your personal life at the door. This is an impossible task for those whose work and home doors became one and the same. Previously blurry lines have all but disappeared for many employees. We've seen each other's kids, pets, and piles of laundry in the background. Welcome to the whole person.

Say goodbye to killing yourself for a career. A growing number of workers have come to the realization that they can't have it all—or at least not all at one time—and are not willing to sacrifice important parts of their lives for a job. Increasingly, people are deciding that work has to work for them.

Say hello to a new way of thinking about how careers happen—through possible moves around, down, up, over...or the decision to strategically develop in place.

Since introducing career development as a rock-climbing adventure rather than an ascent up an imaginary ladder, many metaphors have been circulated. Lattices. Jungle gyms. Squiggly lines. Take your pick. We're sticking with rock climbing because there's still a lot of wisdom and opportunities for growth to be gleaned from the wall.

Climbing Wall Wisdom 1—The top doesn't have to be the goal. Not everyone can reach it. And not everyone wants it.

I'm happy at my current level. I don't ever want the headaches of being the boss. But I also don't want to stagnate where I am. I need to keep figuring out the next challenge, the next place I can make things happen.

—Technician

Climbing Wall Wisdom 2—There are lots of ways around. Countless paths are available to get from point A to point B.

I've reinvented myself several times over my career. Moving from sales to operations and now to customer service sure wasn't the straightest path, but I picked up exactly what I needed along the way.

—Customer service supervisor

Climbing Wall Wisdom 3—Sometimes a step back moves you forward. Getting to your ultimate destination might require a counterintuitive move down the wall a bit.

I really wanted to work in product development but knew I'd never be successful (or even considered) because I hadn't spent time in the trenches with the customer. So I consciously downgraded my job title to get the experience that I needed. And it all paid off in the end.

—Product manager

The career-climbing **wall** is **expansive**, offering a wide selection of spots to **explore** and **enjoy**, and a nearly **unlimited combination** of moves in every direction—around, up, over, and down toward one's vision of career success.

Climbing Wall Wisdom 4—Outside conditions inform your choices. You can opt for safer or riskier moves depending upon other factors (like workload, family obligations, energy level, and support).

> *When my youngest child became ill, I knew I couldn't keep up with the demands of my business development group. I had to make a decision. I'm grateful that my manager was open to helping me find another position with more regular hours. Now that everything is settled at home again, I'm happy to be back to my previous frenetic pace.*
>
> —Director, business development

Climbing Wall Wisdom 5—Depending upon your choice of handholds and footholds, you can cultivate strength, skill, and interest without making a move.

> *In my business, there's an overwhelming number of tools, instruments, and different client needs. When I master where I am now and feel ready for the next challenge, I won't need to change roles. I'll just turn my attention to getting up to speed on the new product line and bringing that into my practice.*
>
> —IT lead

ADVANCING THE NOTION OF ADVANCEMENT

The climbing wall metaphor only works if we shift our mindset about what career development, progression, and advancement really mean in today's environment.

We've been brainwashed into thinking that *advancement* means moving up in the organization: taking on more responsibility, managing larger staffs, and earning more money. But that's changing.

Onward and **upward**

has been replaced by

forward and **toward.**

Advancement today—particularly given changing workforce senti-
ments and the heightened importance of such things as meaning, balance, and autonomy—means something different. It means moving
forward and toward one's very personal definition of career success—
which in many cases requires no movement at all.

Do you know

► How your employees define career success?

► What kind of work they want to be doing?

► What they want to achieve?

► What talents they yearn to leverage or activate?

WHAT ABOUT YOU?

Challenge your own mindset and advance your personal notion of
advancement by asking yourself the same questions:

► How do you define career success for yourself?

► What kind of work do you want to be doing?

► What do you want to achieve?

► What talents do you yearn to leverage or activate?

You're in good company if you struggled with your own answers.
You're in even better company if you don't know how your employees
would answer. So is it any wonder that career development is challenging? Most leaders are flying blind.

Employees need to come to terms with how they personally define
career success and recast that as *advancement*. And they need to let you
in on that secret if they want your help and support.

As a result, some of the most important conversations you'll have
with employees involve clarifying their definition of career success.
A profound and thoughtful dialogue can be sparked by asking simple
questions, such as:

► What do you want to be doing?

► How do you want to be doing it?

► With whom and under what circumstances?

There is simply no cookie-cutter approach for the customized, personalized, tailored, just-for-me plan that advances each employee's unique career goals.

This is the part where you're thinking, *I knew this would eventually come around to all the work I have to do to manage my employees' careers. Right?* Wrong.

Let's be clear: It's your job to facilitate the conversations that inspire insights, awareness, and action on the part of the employees. You take the lead in the talk—asking, guiding, reflecting, exploring. But they own the action.

Sideways isn't sidelined.

UP, DOWN, AND ALL AROUND

Understanding each employee's definition of career success is the first step. Pursuing that definition can happen through any number of moves in a variety of different directions. Getting there may mean

- ► Promotions to higher positions

- ► Lateral adjustments

- ► Steps that deliver valuable experience that in the past might have been considered down or backward

- ► Alternative working arrangements such as shifting to contractor, consultant, part-time, or other contingent employment status

- ► The strategic choice to grow in place

Up is what immediately comes to most people's minds when they think about career advancement. And, although there may be fewer opportunities closer to the top, vertical moves remain important and necessary. Organizations thrive when they have a pipeline filled with skilled internal candidates prepared to take on the challenges of the next level.

But up is not the only way to go for employees looking for growth. In fact, in these days of flatter organizations, other sources of internal mobility offer potent opportunities for development and engagement, as well as the benefit of talent retention.

For instance, a lateral move can become the new promotion.

Increasingly, becoming knowledgeable about more of the organization is seen as an asset. Taking on a role at a similar level on the org chart broadens perspective. It encourages a more holistic view of the business. It activates a new and expanded network. And it builds agility.

Recalibration is another option, although it won't win popularity contests with employees. How can you help others understand that moving from one level to another that may be considered lower organizationally is valid, honorable, and frequently strategic? (Answer: begin by believing it yourself.)

Leaders have to help employees see that it's not **down shifting**.

It's just **changing lanes**, sometimes avoiding the traffic, and seeing **new scenery** in the process.

Sometimes the smartest move—and the fastest way forward—is to intentionally step back.

> *I saw the writing on the wall. My division had a first-class ticket to outsourcing. I wanted to stay with the company—so I moved over to another division and from managing three people to being an individual contributor again. My ego took a hit for a while. But I established myself quickly and learned a lot. It was exactly what I needed to get me where I am today.*
>
> **—Engineer**

It can be a hard sell—but recalibration is frequently the best way for employees to progress forward toward their goals. (There's also the option of growing in place. But this option is so rich and filled with opportunities that it gets its own chapter...so read on.)

Clearly, *up* is not the only way. And even if up is the preferred destination, the climbing wall—the business environment in which we all operate—offers lots of interesting ways to get there.

WHAT'S YOUR DEVELOPMENT DISPOSITION?

It happens all the time (or we hope it does). An employee's skills and experience increase to the point that they need challenges no longer available within their current role.

Leader A begins to sweat and scrambles to hold on to their talent (talent they've invested in developing) by any means possible. Leader B embraces the opportunities associated with internal mobility and actively facilitates the employee's next steps within the organization.

What's the difference between the two? Their development disposition.

Leader A exhibits a scarcity mindset. They believe that their talent belongs to them and think narrowly in terms of their department's needs. Unfortunately, this can lead to dangerous outcomes, including talent hoarding, disengagement, and the loss of the very employee Leader A was so desperately trying to hang on to.

By contrast, Leader B views talent as an enterprise-wide resource and approaches an employee's growth with a sense of abundance. They recognize that they don't own talent; they just rent it for a time. They generously help people find other opportunities. That's because they view talent as

Wouldn't you rather lose a top performer to a colleague down the **hallway**...

than to a competitor down the **highway**?

an enterprise resource. Sharing an employee with a colleague or other department isn't viewed as a loss but rather as a win for the organization.

Is Leader B disappointed to give up a key player? Sure. But they appreciate that they are part of something bigger than themselves. They realize that their commitment to development contributes not just to their team but to the organization as a whole. And they quickly learn that their reputation for helping others grow makes them a talent magnet, capable of attracting a steady stream of new team members to backfill those who've moved on.

Internal mobility highlights, celebrates, and circulates hidden potential within the organization. And while it might feel inconvenient in the short term, the alternative is unwanted turnover with all of its long-term implications.

WHAT ABOUT YOU?

Consider your own development disposition. Mark the word in each row that best describes your feelings and behavior.

Leader A	Leader B
Grudging	Generous
Stingy	Selfless
Cheap	Charitable
All about me	Abundant

If you find yourself leaning toward the right column, congratulations. Your disposition allows you to develop and share your talent generously within the organization, contributing to internal mobility and the new challenges (and heightened retention) that come with it. If you find yourself leaning toward the left column, all we can say is: Be like Leader B.

What IF...

▶ you had a clear understanding of how each employee uniquely defines career success?

▶ employees experienced career advancement and development more like a rock-climbing wall than a ladder?

▶ talent really became an enterprise-wide resource?

- -

Same Seat,
NEW VIEW

My friend worked for the same boss in the same department for nearly seven years. Sounds mind numbing, right? For him, it was anything but. His manager encouraged him to keep changing it up, helped him develop and really use his talents in all sorts of new ways. He grew way more than I did, even changing jobs every couple of years. That's the kind of manager I want.

—An employee (perhaps yours)

Be honest. All that talk of insight, possibilities, recalibration, and upward and lateral moves in the last chapter made you a little nervous, didn't it? As much as you'd like to help your employees transition into new roles that will support their growth goals, it's not always possible. And that's why too many managers avoid career discussions altogether. You don't want to set unrealistic expectations only to disappoint when desirable moves are few and far between.

THINK GLOBAL, ACT LOCAL

Hindsight and foresight overlap to reveal insights into a whole world of development possibilities that exist for employees. Some involve moves. But here's the best-kept secret that will liberate development-minded leaders everywhere: the vast majority do not.

Growth is not now and has never been limited to movements over, up, or down. But somehow that expectation has gotten a lot more air-time than it deserves. With the right support, people can grow right where they're planted.

Growth in place is the most accessible yet most underused career development strategy available to leaders. Let's face it. You may have little influence over getting an employee transferred or promoted, but you are completely in charge of what goes on in your own backyard.

Finding ways to grow talents, explore interests, and build capacity within the context of one's current job is completely within your sphere of influence.

Do you want to

► Raise engagement levels?

► Uncover and activate previously unknown or underused talents that can help the business?

► Retain top talent by keeping work interesting?

► Establish a culture of continuous learning and development?

► Boost the level of connection and belonging?

► Build the skills and knowledge needed so employees will be prepared when broader moves become available?

► Generate loyalty and the kind of leadership reputation that will have the best talent standing in line to work for you?

You can help employees move forward and toward their career goals without making a move. Help them grow in place. But making this happen requires a shift in mindset.

TANGLED IN TITLES

Remember as a kid how adults were always asking what you wanted to *be* when you grew up? Astronaut. Designer. Doctor. We've been programmed since childhood to think in terms of *being*. And this is reinforced in the workplace by the org chart—sending us to chase after a progression of positions and titles.

But we know that given today's reality, there simply may not be that many positions or titles available. And roles we might aspire to today could disappear tomorrow, replaced by jobs that we haven't even imagined. Does it mean that people who remain in the same role are condemned to pickling their minds, extinguishing their spirits, and not developing? Absolutely not.

What do you want to ~~be~~ do?

What it means is that leaders must shift the conversation from what employees want to *be* to what they want to *do*.

► What kind of work do you want to be doing?

► What problems do you want to solve?

► What challenges do you want to confront?

► What kinds of materials, issues, or customers do you want to deal with?

► What achievements do you want to attain?

► What legacy do you want to leave?

The challenge of growing in place involves stripping titles from our thinking and instead focusing on what the employee needs to experience, know, learn, and be able to do.

When you **reframe** development as co-creating enriching experiences, you widen the lens of **possibilities** and allow your people to **grow** right where they are.

I figured out a long time ago that the job title doesn't mean nearly as much as the richness of the experiences it offers. Titles belong on books—not on people.

—Retail supervisor

Discussions around what people want to be are inherently limiting. There will likely never be enough promotions and moves to go around. But discussions about what people want to do are constrained only by the creativity that you and the employee bring to them. Effective leaders can always find ways to invite greater challenge and interest into the envelope of someone's current role.

Focusing more on *doing* and less on *being* offers employees the opportunity to expand their definitions of career success in ways that allow for greater development in place. This mindset acknowledges the reality of the current workplace while meeting the needs of the employee and the organization at the same time.

Managers who successfully support others growing in place are opportunity minded. Are you?

WHAT ABOUT YOU? - - - - - - - - - - - - - - - - -

Do you

See people as interesting, complex, and multidimensional?	☐ YES	☐ NO
Pick up on cues that employees are ready for something more?	☐ YES	☐ NO
Spot strengths that can be used in different or unusual ways?	☐ YES	☐ NO
See multiple ways of getting work done?	☐ YES	☐ NO
Squeeze learning from nearly every experience and interaction?	☐ YES	☐ NO
Cringe when you hear someone say, "But that's not how we do it around here"?	☐ YES	☐ NO
View job descriptions as helpful guidelines rather than handcuffs?	☐ YES	☐ NO
Take pleasure in finding ways to maximize talent?	☐ YES	☐ NO
Feel energized by thinking outside of the box?	☐ YES	☐ NO
Resist seeing the world in terms of round pegs and square holes?	☐ YES	☐ NO

Analysis

► If you answered *yes* eight or more times, you are an opportunity visionary with 20/20 vision when it comes to finding ways to help employees seek out the circumstances they need to gain important skills, knowledge, and experiences.

- ▶ If you answered *yes* five to seven times, you are opportunity minded and frequently see ways to connect your employees' career needs with possibilities within the organization.

- ▶ If you answered *yes* four or fewer times, you may find that you are turning a blind eye toward opportunities to help your employees grow.

It was a head scratcher at first. My technical documentation specialist announced that she wanted to become a nonprofit grant writer—not something our manufacturing team needed. But after thinking about it together, we identified several skill areas shared by both roles. We figured out that developing her writing skills would improve her current projects and prepare her for creating grants. She also helped writing proposals and other influence pieces for sales. As a result, her engagement and commitment grew—and now she does some volunteer grant writing on the side.

—Documentation manager

Opportunity-minded managers envision and enable **possibility-advancing** circumstances with employees— through **conversation**.

Opportunity is defined as a set of circumstances that makes it possible to do something—in this case, it involves helping others move forward and toward their definition of career success while finding ways to do what interests them most.

But even opportunity-minded leaders fall prey to an all-too-common mistake. They jump directly from employees' definitions of success or descriptions of what they want to do to "Here's what we're gonna do." It's natural. As a leader, you didn't get to where you are by not being action oriented. But sometimes this bias for action can backfire.

Moving prematurely to action causes you to shoehorn the possible into the practical far too early. It also

► Side steps important thinking

► Chokes off creativity

► Jumps to solutions before you know what the opportunity is

► Narrows the conversation

► Blinds you to the full range of possibilities

So instead slow down a bit. Explore what the employees need to know or be capable of so they can *do* what interests them most. Consider the skills, information, and abilities that will enable success. Crystallize these needs and priorities before jumping to action.

► TRY THIS: FIRST THINGS FIRST
- -

Agree with the employee that you'll both suspend all talk of how to achieve what's needed. Instead, focus jointly on determining what is required for helping your employee move forward. Questions like these open up the possibilities:

  ► To reach your goal, what skills and knowledge will you need?

  ► How can you get ready for what you want to do?

  ► What capabilities will prepare you to be successful?

► What gaps might currently exist?

► What do you need to learn?

► What skills might you want to acquire?

► What might you need more of?

► What might you need less of?

What you're looking for during this conversation are these kinds of responses:

► I need to broaden my business exposure.

► I've got to get more experience in different situations.

► I'd really benefit from getting closer to the customer.

► Developing a global perspective—that's what I need.

► I need to get some P&L responsibility under my belt.

► Can you help me create a strong support network?

► I'll have to increase the complexity of the leadership challenges I face.

What you're *not* looking for are these kinds of responses:

► I have to manage the customer care department.

► You've got to transfer me to John's group.

► Please enroll me in the next management training series.

► I'd like your job, thanks for asking.

These sorts of responses are signals that the employee is jumping to solutions before fully exploring the problem, opportunity, or gap.

Together, generate a broad pool of skills, abilities, and information that will help employees move forward and toward their definitions of success. Opportunity-minded leaders know how to make this happen.

GOAL SETTING: IN A WORD

In the brave new world of redefining career success, focusing on what people want to do versus what they want to be, and leveraging one's role for development, many of the old rules of goal setting no longer apply. Leaders need to let go of the comfort of prescribed pathways, tidy trajectories, and "*b* must follow *a*" thinking. Role-based goals must give way to something more organic and, as it turns out, something even simpler.

Want to set a new kind of goal that's not necessarily anchored in positions? Pick a word. The In-Role Goal Generator is a collection of powerful words—words that are synonymous with growth.

They get people thinking more creatively and expansively. They point employees in new and sometimes invisible directions. They establish or maintain momentum forward and toward the employee's career goals. This list is just the beginning!

► TRY THIS: FIRE UP THE GENERATOR

- -

1. Share the In-Role Goal Generator with employees to spark thinking about the skills, capabilities, experiences, and information required to move forward and toward their definitions of career success, which involves doing what interests them most.

2. Ask employees to pick as many words as apply and to use them as starters for phrases that describe what they need or want. (Examples: "I need to broaden my network of resources to include more engineers" or "I want to sharpen my presentation skills—particularly with more senior and skeptical audiences.") Don't settle for generic responses; work together to get specific statements that will advance the employee's interests.

3. Based upon your understanding of their interests, have a few ideas in your hip pocket and questions that might help guide the employee if necessary.

In-Role Goal Generator

- ☐ Strengthen
- ☐ Enhance
- ☐ Cultivate
- ☐ Expand
- ☐ Increase
- ☐ Sharpen
- ☐ Specialize
- ☐ Raise
- ☐ Intensify
- ☐ Multiply
- ☐ Deepen
- ☐ Refresh
- ☐ Revive
- ☐ Test
- ☐ Experiment
- ☐ Practice
- ☐ Seek
- ☐ Learn
- ☐ Communicate
- ☐ Share
- ☐ Observe
- ☐ Look
- ☐ Add
- ☐ Reconsider
- ☐ Minimize
- ☐ Decrease

4. Discuss each word chosen and the phrase it inspired. Clarify and identify additional details.

Approaching the conversation in this way reframes opportunities for development, moving away from titles and promotions and toward a more doable focus. It offers fodder for growth in the here and now, leveraging the current role rather than waiting for some future promotion that might or might not come. It offers meaningful growth to those who are looking for a different or richer relationship with their work. And it enriches the experience, engagement, and growth of those employees who—perhaps not interested in a promotion—might have passed on the opportunity for development in the past.

WHAT ABOUT YOU?

Which words appeal to you? What ideas do they prompt around what you need or want to develop your own career?

This is how you use what's completely within your control and sphere of influence—and within the employee's current role—to offer a personalized development experience that allows people to see a brand-new view without ever having to move.

What IF...

▶ employees expanded their career thinking beyond a litany of roles and titles?

▶ everyone became even just a little more opportunity minded?

▶ developing in place became as attractive, interesting, exciting, and respected as other options?

— 8 —

Advancing
ACTION

We go through the exercise every year. Spend a bunch of time figuring out what I need to develop my career. Time's typically up just about when we get around to how to make it happen. I honestly think this does more harm than good. It's like a tease that gives me a hint of what's possible then slams the door on it—until next year, when we do it all over again.

—An employee (perhaps yours)

The work you do with employees around hindsight and foresight helps generate insight into the world of possibilities that exists for those who want to move forward and toward their career goals. Identifying those possibilities is exciting and energizing—whether they involve preparing for a move or developing in place. But those possibilities remain high level and abstract until they're translated into action.

This translation doesn't happen magically or by chance. Rather, it happens through intentional effort—and intentional conversation between you and your employees.

Whether your employees wish to refresh their knowledge of a technical system, practice new work processes, sharpen their ability to identify the best deals, extend their knowledge of one product line to another, strengthen interpersonal skills, or any other developmental priority, you have three primary ways to make it happen.

▶ TRY THIS

- -

To learn more about the developmental strategies available to you (and your own go-to preferences), consider the range of activities that support learning.

Circle the three or four approaches you have used most frequently and effectively to learn and to grow.

A
BOOKS AND ARTICLES

LIVE WORKSHOPS

E-LEARNING OR WEBINARS

PODCASTS

B
INFORMATION INTERVIEWS

OBSERVING OTHERS
NETWORKING

MENTORING

JOB SHADOWING

C
SPECIAL PROJECTS

JOB ROTATION
STRETCH ASSIGNMENTS

COMMUNITY SERVICE

ACTION LEARNING
(THROUGH PROJECTS/TEAMS)

The developmental activities you've gravitated toward in the past fall within one of three broad categories—known as the 3 Es—that are available for you to use with your employees. Were you drawn toward a majority of items in one category? Or did you choose activities from two or all three of the Es?

A. **EDUCATION**—the ever-expanding sources of information and learning opportunities that can be formally or informally accessed.

B. **EXPOSURE**—the opportunities to learn from and through others via observation, mentorship, and more.

C. **EXPERIENCE**—action-based opportunities to learn by doing.

Understanding and using all of these strategies will allow you to work with employees to move from development insights and ideas to implementation.

EDUCATION: BACK TO SCHOOL (SORT OF)

When people think of learning and development, they naturally think of education. For the majority of us, school is where we got most of our instruction and did most of our growing up.

In the workplace, education takes many forms—both old school and new school in nature. There are workshops (in-person and virtual) on nearly any topic you can imagine. Community colleges offer credit and noncredit courses to build necessary knowledge and skills.

But with education no longer limited to live-group settings, learning has been democratized. Opportunities are ubiquitous for individuals to access what they need when they need it through platforms like LinkedIn Learning, millions of hours of instructional video, AI, and virtual support. A nearly unlimited selection of resources is available 24/7 for just-in-time, just-for-me learning.

► TRY THIS: ENABLE EDUCATION

It's easy to assume that if you've pointed employees in the right direction—or even connected them to the learning resources—your role is over. After all, it's up to them. Right? Wrong. People get the most value from education when their leaders help set them up for success. You'll see the best results if you follow these steps.

1. Clarify the learning outcomes and commitment to achieve them. Through conversation, you can help employees focus their effort and attention for optimal results. You can do this with questions like

    ► How will this learning opportunity help move you forward and toward your career goals?

    ► What specifically do you hope to gain?

    ► How will you use what you've learned?

    ► What challenges or obstacles might come up as you learn?

    ► How will you address these challenges or obstacles?

    ► What are you willing to invest to make the most of this learning opportunity?

    ► What do you need from me? (This one's optional, but only because many managers are afraid this will lead to a lengthy list of to-dos. Just try it. You'll be amazed at the small requests that can lead to disproportionately large returns on learning.)

2. Treat education like the real work that it is. Scheduling employees into an instructional opportunity is easy. Preserving that time so they can focus on the learning at hand—that's tougher. Nothing says "Your education and development don't matter" any louder than pulling people out of seminars, interrupting webinars, or letting other priorities preempt learning commitments. In fact, one of the biggest employee complaints is the discrepancy between what managers say about their commitment to learning and their behavior.

3. Co-create opportunities for employees to use what they've learned. New skills and knowledge must be exercised to grow strong. So partner before, during, and after the educational experiences to find meaty and meaningful ways people can apply, extend, and strengthen their learning.

4. Set a date to debrief. (More on this later.)

Training used to be the panacea for everything. But with budget cuts and production pressures, leaders are being more thoughtful about how to get the biggest bang from their employees' investment of time and money in training. They're getting more involved on the front end and the back end. And I think it's really paying off.

—Training director

EXPOSURE: WISDOM IN THE WORKPLACE

By now, you've probably learned the refrain of this book by heart: you don't have to do it all. And that applies here. You can facilitate exposure simply by facilitating connections. The more individuals who are drawn into an employee's career support circle, the better.

Once I realized that even if I had all the time in the world, I couldn't be all things to all people, it took a lot of pressure off. There are so many other people in the organization who are much better suited to help my folks learn what they need to know.

—Sales manager

Enabling exposure through mentoring, job shadowing, coaching, and networking costs virtually nothing. It can efficiently deliver development—while building opportunities for connection, belonging, and a range of other positive outcomes. The key is to help employees determine who are the best resources available. Start the dialogue with questions like:

▶ Who's known for...?

▶ Which groups or teams have experience with...?

▶ Whose work do you admire in the area of...?

▶ Who might know someone who can help you learn more about...?

▶ Who's demonstrated skills and abilities around...?

WIN-WIN SCENARIO

When employees are looking to learn and grow, they frequently focus on what they can get. That makes sense, but sometimes the most profound learning comes from what they can give.

In the past, mentoring was often conceived as a one-way, one-on-one transaction in which a more knowledgeable individual passed along wisdom, guidance, and insights around a body of knowledge to someone in need of learning. But in today's dynamic business environment, many people are challenging that old conception because

▶ Nobody knows it all. As a result, employees should strive to develop the broadest network possible of connections from whom they can learn. The past structure of one mentor to one protégé is history. The new model looks more like a mosaic of connections.

▶ It's reciprocal. Given the diversity in the workplace, there is something to be learned from nearly everyone we encounter. Enlightened mentors can learn as much as they teach.

My investment in mentoring younger associates is completely selfish. I might have more case experience and a deeper understanding of the law, but that's it. They have entirely new methods for researching and organizing data that I'm trying to master. They aren't mired in the way we've always done things around here—and are always teaching me something new. I get way more than I give in these relationships.

—Attorney/senior partner

Teaching is sometimes the best way to learn. Progressive educators have known this for decades. So employees should look not just for people they can learn from but also for those who can learn from *them*. Lessons in human dynamics, leadership, and communication are just the beginning.

Exposure in the form of mentoring, job shadowing, and networking is all about creating compelling connections among individuals who can share knowledge, skills, and experience. These individuals could be peers, superiors, subordinates, people in other departments, or people outside the organization altogether. As a leader, you can open the door—and even your contact lists—but the employee has to walk through and take it from there.

EXPERIENCE: ENGINEER OPPORTUNITIES

Education and exposure go a long way toward helping employees develop. But experience is frequently the best and most powerful teacher. Ask any five employees about the most important lessons they've learned and how they learned them. We predict that more than half didn't happen through education, training, or even other people. The key lessons came from people's experiences—in many cases, the school of hard knocks.

WHAT ABOUT YOU?

List the five most significant lessons you've learned. Trace each lesson back to where and when you learned it. How many were a result of education or exposure? If you're like most people, the vast majority of your learning has come through experience.

Experience-based learning is the Holy Grail for which many managers have been searching. Most people learn by doing. And there's a lot that needs to be done at work. Strategically bring the two together (someone with a learning need and authentic work assignments), and you can simultaneously serve the needs of the organization and the individual: a match made in heaven.

Experience-based learning is about integrating learning into the workflow. Some call it *embedded*; we just call it a sensible way to efficiently and effectively develop the talents of others.

On-the-job learning is my personal favorite...in part due to its efficiency. Employees get what they need, and at the same time, we accomplish real work that matters.

—Finance supervisor

Experience-based learning can sound daunting. But don't be put off by it. Sending employees abroad or starting a new division for someone to head up are certainly experiences. But that's not what we're talking about here.

Scale experiences based on your sphere of influence, organizational needs, and what employees want to achieve.

You have plenty of simple, doable options available to you right now—in fact, unlimited options—when you consider combinations and permutations of

▶ Stretch assignments

▶ Special projects

▶ Events

▶ In-department rotations

▶ Action learning projects and teams

▶ Employee resource groups (ERGs)

▶ Community service and volunteer efforts

The most potent and valuable development experiences involve hands-on, in-the-moment learning. There's no substitute for being confronted by and having to address real business challenges. And, given the number of challenges facing businesses today, the opportunity to leverage them is limited only by the imagination. Here are some examples.

If the development priority is to . . .	The experience might include . . .
▶ enhance understanding of how customers use the product or service	▶ conducting customer interviews, generating a summary report, and presenting findings at a department meeting
▶ cultivate supervisory and coaching skills	▶ working with all new hires to set expectations, develop job skills, and provide feedback and coaching
▶ broaden exposure to the challenges of delivering services in another territory	▶ standing in for an employee in another office while he or she is on leave

THE ZEN OF EXPERIENTIAL LEARNING

Without getting too deep, there are three truths that a manager must confront before helping people learn through experiences.

► With intention and attention, nearly any experience can drive learning and development. The activity doesn't need to be big or flashy. In fact, it can be quite small and insignificant. But learning is possible if the employee is focused on making it happen and reflecting on the lessons.

► There's no such thing as failure in a learning experience—only failure to learn from it. The quality of the outcome has little to do with the quality of the learning. In fact, according to some experts, humans learn more (and more quickly) through hardships and failure. The key is to help employees wring every bit of insight and learning from the experiences they have.

► Learning is a choice. And it's not yours. Employees must decide to actively engage and learn. You can help them think through how to do it, but they must take responsibility for the hard work of learning.

Ninety percent of great career-advancing ideas go nowhere. Don't let your employees' efforts suffer that fate. Push the ideas just a little bit further, enough to make your conversations pay off.

DEALING UP DEVELOPMENT RESULTS

Whatever combination of education, exposure, and experience you and your employee arrive at, there needs to be a plan—a plan that's hatched together through conversation. And the best plans are really collaborative development deals you strike with the employee. Make sure your DEAL is documented, employee owned, aligned with their goals, and linked to the needs of your organization.

Documented. Putting it in writing signals that this is significant and that you both are taking it seriously. It acts as a reminder to you and the employee and helps to drive follow-up. Write it on paper or electronically rather than in concrete. Agility is the name of the game, so treat the plan as the living, breathing, and changeable tool that it is.

Employee owned. If they don't have buy-in, you might as well opt out. Employees must take responsibility for their plans and generate the commitment and energy required to implement them. Ownership skyrockets when a plan is personalized to the individual, focused, specific, and doable in light of other activities.

Aligned with the employee's goals. Linking the plan to short-term and long-term goals tests whether activities are worth the effort they will take. When the going gets tough, this overt link can help the employee sustain focus and energy to push forward and toward their bigger career objectives.

Linked to the needs of the organization. Let's get real. Resources are in short supply and support can be fickle. Both can be pulled at any time. Don't jeopardize your development efforts. If what employees are doing to learn and develop contributes directly to the bigger picture, you are on safe and solid ground.

SEAL THE DEAL

Development activity is only that—activity—until it is properly unpacked to reveal its lessons. In fact, many employees become so engaged in the experience that they don't take the time to reflect on how they've benefited from it. Yet again, conversation becomes the key to genuine growth, and simple questions help you launch dialogue that unpacks learning.

► What did you learn from that?   ► In what ways were you chal-
                                      lenged or stretched?

- ▶ What pitfalls or obstacles did you discover?

- ▶ What guidelines or principles did you derive?

- ▶ Why were you successful? Or not?

- ▶ How can you use your learning/insight in the future?

- ▶ What would you do differently?

- ▶ How can you use your learning/insight in other contexts?

- ▶ What did you discover about yourself in the process?

- ▶ What will you take away from this?

Just one or two of these questions can guide employees toward turning the experience into development.

But keep in mind that this sort of debriefing isn't the exclusive domain of the leader. Peers can help unpack learning among themselves and hold each other accountable. Alternately, skip-level conversations can be powerful, allowing employees to meet, get to know, and gain insights from your leader.

In fact, someone on your team may be looking to develop the ability to coach and help others grow. Wouldn't debriefing another team member's learning be a great development experience for them? Remember, development opportunities are ever present and limited only by your own imagination.

Interesting, meaningful, and exciting possibilities emerge from the hindsight, foresight, and insight conversations you have with employees. But leader beware: If you and your employee identify these possibilities and then fail to implement them, trust, engagement, and job satisfaction are likely to fall lower than if you'd never had the conversation in the first place.

But this negative result is completely unnecessary because leaders have three powerful ways to translate abstract inklings into tangible developmental action: through education, exposure, and experience.

A **few minutes** of **conversation** can help others slow down enough to **reflect**, bring deep insights to the surface, **verbalize** important messages, and consider how to **leverage** their expanding skills and knowledge base.

What IF...

▶ everyone in the organization consciously looked for what they could learn from others as well as what they could teach others?

▶ every employee was committed to at least one development action that was documented, aligned with their goals, and linked to the needs of the organization?

▶ development activities were considered incomplete until employees had a chance to reflect on and discuss what they learned?

Grow with the **FLOW**

For me, it doesn't have to be a big sit-down meeting. In fact, I'd rather it wasn't. Doesn't it seem odd that something as important and personal as someone's career is put on an annual schedule...sort of like a termite inspection?

—An employee (perhaps yours)

Want real results? Take career development off the calendar and bring it into real everyday life.

We understand the reality. Many organizations feel the need for individual development planning (IDP) schedules and processes to ensure that career conversations happen—and happen equitably. For some employees, it's the only time during the year that a development dialogue might occur. And yet, despite organizational mandates and efforts, our research indicates that nearly 20 percent of those polled don't get even that "annual inspection."

As many businesses are rethinking event-based performance management processes in favor of more frequent and ongoing interactions, it's only natural for career development to follow.

Don't get us wrong—we're all for the regular, planned career conversations. (We've even prepared an online resource to help you wring the most value from IDPs: visit help-them-grow.com/resources.) But on their own, in isolation, as the only time leaders and managers address growth, they just don't cut it. Annual conversations don't allow development to operate at and respond to the speed of business. And they don't meet today's employees' need for real and regular attention to their growth.

This is why effective leaders embrace ongoing development planning, or ODP (IDP's more inclusive cousin).

SUPPLEMENT THE SCHEDULED WITH THE SPONTANEOUS

What's needed is a more contemporary, organic, and effective way to supplement the scheduled with the spontaneous—to build a development relationship and to weave growth into the eternally evolving fabric of the workplace.

Consider the differences between these approaches:

Traditional IDP	vs.	Inclusive ODP
Taking it all offline: Saving it all up for that annual discussion (which may be eleven months and three weeks away).		Operating in real time: Connecting in the moment when something's going on, emotions are fresh, and receptivity is heightened.
Artificial exchanges: Mandated conversations during which leaders and employees work through forms and scripts.		Authentic exchanges: Genuine conversations, based on real and immediate stimulus within the workplace.
One and done: A batched approach to addressing career issues, where thirsty people are expected to drink from a firehose and make it last another year.		Iterative interaction: A layered approach in which information unfolds in digestible chunks, allowing insights and plans to build incrementally over time and growth to occur step by doable step.

Call it what you will: In the moment. On the spot. Context-sensitive. Instant. Bite-size. On the fly. Impromptu. Nano-coaching. Stealth development. We call it growing with the flow—workflow, that is. And it's an essential supplement and complement to traditional individual development planning.

I learned years ago that career development happens on its own schedule. The annual meeting is nice…but I use it more as a chance to summarize and capture highlights. I try to position myself to be there to support others throughout the year when real development—or the chance for it—occurs.

—Small business banker

DROP IN FOR DEVELOPMENT

Growing with the flow means development isn't limited to scheduled meetings. As a result, it becomes less burdensome in many ways. It can be quick—as short as one or two minutes. It can be casual—right on the shop floor or while waiting for others to join a virtual call. It can be completely unplanned—no notes or agendas to contend with. Hardly sounds like work, right?

But in life, there are always trade-offs. When you help others grow with the flow, you can save time and do it with less planning. But you've got to be willing to give something as well. And that something is a little more of your attention.

This approach places a new and non-negotiable demand upon leaders. It requires that you heighten your sensitivity to the cues around you. It requires being present and in the moment. It requires noticing and acting upon opportunities as they arise.

Yet, when you think about it, being cue-sensitive is nothing more than a variation on the theme of curiosity.

Cue sensitivity is **curiosity** in **action.**

If you're cultivating curiosity in your conversations, it's not a huge leap to bring curiosity to the world around you. To pick up on what's going on under the surface. To look at situations and events ready to ask "What can we learn from this?" To see the world around you as fodder for development.

CATCH A CUE

Sometimes you can learn more about a concept by studying it from an unusual angle. Along those lines, we've surveyed thousands of individuals across industries and asked them to share examples of times when their leaders *missed* important career conversation cues.

Which cues from the following list do you think might have come up in our results?

- ► The employee expresses an interest in learning something new.
- ► Job responsibilities or expectations change.
- ► The employee shares a concern or lack of confidence.
- ► A new project launches.
- ► An old project ends.
- ► Uncertainty is affecting the industry or organization.
- ► The employee takes on a new opportunity or assignment.
- ► The employee is passed over for an opportunity or assignment.
- ► New credentials or awards are earned.
- ► The employee inquires about an opportunity.
- ► A high-profile failure occurs.
- ► Low-profile errors are made.
- ► The employee demonstrates extra effort or interest.
- ► Effort appears to be trailing off.

▶ The employee shares something interesting they've read, seen, or heard.

▶ Milestones are met.

▶ Milestones are missed.

▶ The employee appears to be struggling.

▶ Things are going poorly.

▶ Things are going well.

Spoiler alert: Don't read further until you've made your guesses.

Real employees—from various roles, levels, and industries—shared every single one of these missed opportunities for development.

WHAT ABOUT YOU?

Review the list again and mark any (it's your book, go ahead, you won't get in trouble) that happened to you over the past week—opportunities for your own manager to initiate a career conversation with you. Then ask yourself which of these might have occurred with your own employees over the past week. How many of these cues did you follow up on with a conversation?

Cues to grow with the flow abound—whether things are going well or poorly. Whether people are hitting or missing deadlines. Whether they're winning or losing. The opportunities to leverage real life for real development are there—if we just develop the habit of looking for them.

PROMOTE A PAUSE

If recognizing a cue is the first step, then what's step two? Cause a pause. Just like tapping the pause button on a digital device, briefly suspend the action so you can take advantage of the opportunity.

Pausing can redirect the **momentum** of the **moment** toward supporting and informing career growth.

Growing with the flow by having unplanned—but still intentional— conversations honors the cadence of business and the authentic, real-time, iterative nature of development. When you spot the cues and cause a pause, you encourage growth not just once a year but day in and day out.

FOCUS YOUR FLOW

Growing with the flow is nothing more than a conversation using the questions and approaches sprinkled throughout this book. You have everything you need to seize the moment and turn an opening into a development opportunity.

Pick a question—any question—that lets you delve into hindsight, foresight, or insight.

If the employee is struggling with a project, help look backward at strengths that contributed to the effort and what additional skills might be required. **(Hindsight)**

It's counterintuitive, but when things aren't going well, that is the best time to focus on strengths. It gives the employee a needed boost and nearly always surfaces something they can tap into to help the situation.

—Scientist/principal investigator

If the employee shares a story from the news about a competitor or concerns about the latest tech advance, explore what that means for your industry and your own organization. **(Foresight)**

It's easy to get sucked into the day-to-day grind. I've got to find every opportunity possible to keep my crew thinking big picture. It helps the hotel, and it helps them as individuals.

—Hospitality team leader

If the employee has completed an assignment that was a stretch, open a conversation about the challenges encountered, what was learned, and how it can be applied. **(Insight)**

Ask a hindsight, foresight, or insight question and you'll have gone a long way toward seizing the moment and infusing career development into daily life. Ask the three question types together, and you have an unbeatable combination.

When you make it a habit to help others grow with the flow, additional benefits follow. Your regularly scheduled career conversations will be richer and more efficient because of the effort you've invested throughout the year. And over time you'll train employees to pick up on their own cues, cause their own pauses, and take greater ownership for driving their own development. The benefits of this kind of growing just keep flowing.

What IF...

► employees felt like their careers were precious gems to be polished frequently over time?

► you were in the habit of leveraging day-to-day life at work toward development?

► annual career conversations were the culmination of growing with the flow throughout the year?

Developing
at a
DISTANCE

My face may be the same size as everyone else's in those boxes on our virtual team meetings, but I sure feel a lot smaller than my colleagues in the office when it comes to developing my career remotely.

—An employee (perhaps yours)

The debate rages on, but remote and hybrid work is here to stay—in some way, shape, or form. Organizations demonstrated that they actually could support a distributed workforce—when they had to. And employees have tasted the productivity and personal benefits that go along with more flexible working conditions. The toothpaste is out of the tube, and forcing it back in has proven to be a messy if not impossible task for those trying to return things to how they used to be.

VEXED BY THE FLEX

The introduction of wide-scale remote and hybrid working relationships has changed your role as a leader enormously. How you meet. How you share information. How you delegate assignments. How you monitor work and progress. How you collaborate. And, perhaps most consequentially (at least from our viewpoint), how you develop employees who are not consistently co-located.

And while—by necessity—most of your regular tasks and processes have been retooled for virtual use, in many organizations, developing employees from a distance has lagged far behind. And for good reason. It comes with a lot of challenges. Which have you seen or experienced?

▶ Unintentional inequity

▶ Assumptions and misconceptions about remote or hybrid workers

▶ Out of sight, out of mind

- ► Communication challenges

- ► Fewer organic, casual opportunities to connect

- ► Loss of nonverbal cues

- ► Failure of many development resources to accommodate virtual workers

Welcome to proximity bias—the human tendency to favor those who are physically present while inadvertently disadvantaging those who aren't. It's a very real form of discrimination that leaders must address and actively guard against.

WHAT ABOUT YOU?

The first step toward combating any bias is becoming aware of it. Use these questions to do a little soul searching within yourself. Discover how your own beliefs and feelings may be influencing your development relationship with virtual employees. Only then can you take conscious steps to ensure an even development playing field for everyone—no matter where they work.

- ► How do you feel about remote and hybrid work/workers…really?

- ► What do reliability and hard work look like to you?

- ► Do you think virtual and on-site employees bring the same level of commitment to their work?

- ► Do you believe virtual employees are as serious about their careers as their on-site colleagues?

- ► What are your level of fluency and comfort with virtual communication?

- ► How might all of this be affecting your behavior toward remote and hybrid employees—even in unconscious or subtle ways?

BEYOND FOMO

Developing at a distance isn't hard just for leaders; employees are struggling as well. For all that they've gained during this transition, remote and hybrid workers have lost a lot too. Organic opportunities for visibility have evaporated. The informal learning that comes from observation and soaking up the vibe of a situation is no longer accessible. What were once off-the-cuff insights, experiences, and conversation topics must now be agendized. Networking requires more planning and effort. As a result, too many virtual employees have gone from the experience of FOMO (fear of missing out) to the ROMO (reality of missing out) on the career development and growth that had previously been available to them.

OUT OF SIGHT, BUT ON YOUR MIND

In an effort to get a clearer picture of what effective virtual career development looks like, we interviewed 25 authors and experts on the subject, as well as leaders charged with developing virtual teams. We asked them about combating proximity bias, overcoming out-of-sight-out-of-mind pitfalls, and making development happen at a distance. We got ready to capture a laundry list of actions to pass along to you. Instead, we heard a consistent refrain—from every single person interviewed.

You've got to do everything you would with on-site employees— only **more intentionally.**

Intention—rather than a litany of new techniques—is the key to helping remote and hybrid employees grow. The advice, questions, and activities in this book offer the essential roadmap you need to develop everyone, no matter where they work. The key is to do it with greater intention virtually.

Start by infusing greater intention into your communication. Being deliberate and purposeful in your conversations sends a message to remote and hybrid employees that their development remains on your radar screen even when you're apart. And it doesn't have to be hard.

We've said it before, and we'll say it again: you're going to be talking with employees anyway. Why not give the conversations an intentional career twist?

Each meeting with a remote team member includes a short discussion about what they've learned or what insights they've had since we spoke last. I ask how they're tracking on their growth goals and what needs to happen to keep those moving forward. I think it sends a strong signal about the importance I place on development.
—Client success director

▶ TRY THIS: REMOTE RITUAL
- -

Set aside 10 minutes at the start of each scheduled meeting to address development. (And by now, you know how to do it and have the questions to make it happen.) Make it a ritual that virtual employees can count on during each one-on-one. Beginning in this way communicates your commitment to their growth and establishes learning as something to draw upon or return to throughout the meeting. (It also ensures that it doesn't get short shrift, as happens too frequently when development is the last agenda item.)

A word of caution. These sorts of rituals have a powerful emotional effect on employees. And they may take on greater importance in the virtual arena.

So don't start unless you're committed to following through consistently. Broken rituals can be more damaging than no rituals at all.

But intention isn't reserved for **words**; it's even more potent in **action**.

Among the greatest disappointments virtual employees report is the experience of losing out on an opportunity because they weren't "in the room where it happened." No judgment here. We get it. Things are moving fast. You're juggling a lot. Passing the ball to someone who's right there is easy and safe. The problem is that it's neither inclusive nor equitable.

A more intentional approach might be to pause, mentally run through the entire team, consider the strengths as well as development needs and goals of each member, then make a reasoned rather than rushed decision—a decision that offers equal opportunity to those who are trying to develop at a distance.

Cultivating the inclusive virtual development culture required to ensure that everyone—no matter where they work—enjoys the growth they want comes down to one key factor: your intention!

▶ TRY THIS: CREATE A GROWTH CHART

Peter Drucker famously said, "What gets measured gets managed." Applied in this context, greater equity and an even development playing field for all requires measuring and managing your own behavior.

1. Draft a roster or chart listing the names of all employees.

2. Each time you have even a casual development conversation with some-one, make a mark.

3. Routinely review the roster to consider your natural, unconscious con-nection trends. Reflect upon the biases that might be driving your behavior.

4. Take action to even things out with more—and more intentional—attention to communicating with those who were underrepresented on the chart.

ORCHESTRATE WHAT'S NOT ORGANIC

Besides long commutes, one of the other major casualties of remote work has been spontaneity. In co-located environments, interactions—including development—happen more naturally and effortlessly. New employees absorb the culture as if by osmosis. A hallway encounter can offer insight into what an employee might need at any given moment. Lessons are freely available to those who simply observe what's going on around them.

Virtual employees don't experience the kind of easy access to organic growth that on-site employees take for granted. This is where intention comes in again—in this case, to compensate for the sponta-neity and serendipity that's less available to those who work remotely. Together, leaders and employees can orchestrate a set of circumstances that might look a little different but still lead to similar, adapted devel-opment opportunities and outcomes. (Think of a book that's made into a movie. The characters and plotline are roughly the same, but some details might need to shift to take advantage of the new medium.)

Sure, the virtual world might not lend itself to chance human encounters. But if, for instance, you and a remote employee are both showing up online in Teams at the same time, why not turn that into an impromptu digital encounter? Check in on how things are going and follow up with a relevant hindsight, foresight, or insight question—just like you would in real life.

Virtual employees can't pop into your office when they'd like to share something or get your take. Instead, one option is batching. Encourage remote employees to keep a journal of wins, challenges, and development discussion topics. Invite them to share what they've captured with you during regular meetings. This practice can offer a rich source of reflection, greater focus when it comes time to discuss it, and learning for everyone. But they certainly don't have to batch it all until your next scheduled meeting. Experiment with how email, text, video, audio messaging, and other technologies might capture the message and energy of the moment—without overburdening either of you.

And if your organization allows for occasional live gatherings of remote employees, agree upon what kinds of development conversations should be reserved for that precious face-to-face time.

WHAT HAPPENED TO WATCHING AND WONDERING?

Think about how much you've learned by silently observing the behavior of others. Why did she say that in that way? How did they arrive at that conclusion? What caused everyone to shift in their chairs when he raised that point? These are the kinds of questions that regularly cycle through the minds of employees who have the benefit of physical presence with others in their organization. And the answers to these questions offer rich context and informal career development.

Given their more limited purview, virtual employees are missing out on opportunities to watch, wonder, and inquire about what's happening in the space they no longer occupy. And this could put newer entrants to the workforce in particular—those who rely on day-to-day modeling to understand the rules of the road—at a distinct disadvantage when it comes to their business maturation and growth. The ability to develop competence in areas like executive presence, cultural compe-

An **invisible curriculum** is missing from the remote employee's **learning plan.**

tence, and interpersonal savvy may be stunted or halted altogether for virtual employees.

Helping virtual employees benefit from the countless workplace cues that inform development requires that leaders add narrator, interpreter, and cultural anthropologist to their job descriptions.

Remote employees need you to **share** what they're not seeing, **translate** events, **decode** dynamics, illuminate nuances, and make cultural sense of it all.

Virtual employees need more context and debriefing than on-site employees to internalize the same insights. So if you want to even the on-site/virtual development playing field, try radical transparency.

Radical transparency isn't about dispensing in-your-face hard truths. It's about leaders looking at the workplace through a new lens. Stepping back from your unconscious level of competence (where interpreting and internalizing important but invisible inputs has likely come to operate on autopilot) to a place of conscious competence where you recognize—and as a result can share with others—subtle cues, undertones, and behaviors that can drive the development of those who can't experience them firsthand.

And don't forget that there's plenty going on in their worlds for which you have limited visibility as well. Turn the tables and invite them to narrate what you can't see. The simple prompt "What am I blind to in your world this week?" or "What do you want me to know that I might not be aware of from a distance?" helps others think more critically about their experience of virtual work—and helps them become better partners in their remote development.

If you're a remote leader, you may need to find your own reliable narrator capable of radical transparency as well.

RETHINK ACCESSIBILITY

When it comes to the experience of development, you can't really "stand in the shoes" of your virtual employees. If you're not working remotely yourself, however, you can certainly sit behind their screens (metaphorically) to develop some understanding and empathy for what life and development is like at a distance.

Have you ever been the only remote participant shoehorned into an otherwise live workshop only to have your participation ignored and contributions marginalized? For many virtual employees, it's all too common. As a leader, you may want to stand in their shoes and audit the experience so you can elevate it with strategies like

► Considering asynchronous learning options that might better suit their needs

► Ensuring that development plans are accessible through collaboration tools to keep everyone on the same digital page

► Creating and encouraging engagement with career development channels on Slack, Teams, or other internal communication vehicles

Making sure that you and your organization provide collaboration tools and remote delivery systems allows virtual employees to own and exercise greater agency over their careers. As they access the development services and resources they need, they'll enjoy the experience of growth they deserve...from anywhere.

ONE HARD TRUTH

This chapter outlines a variety of considerations as well as actions you can take to level the playing field and enable equitable development regardless of where employees may work. But the truth is that in some organizations, career advancement and remote work cannot coexist. Some executives have decided that physical presence and proximity to headquarters are prerequisites for career growth through moves and promotions. (We won't editorialize, but we might judge…just a little.)

If this is your culture, employees who wish to move up or around need to hear this hard truth. Don't sidestep or sugar coat it. They deserve to understand reality so they can make the best decisions about their career. We know it's scary. You might lose them. But isn't it better to lose them now with integrity rather than read about it down the line on Glassdoor?

► TRY THIS: DISTANCE DEVELOPMENT DEBRIEF

Because most of us haven't cracked the code on developing at a distance, it can be helpful to calibrate your efforts. Set aside time to jointly consider questions like these with remote and hybrid employees:

1. To what extent is your experience of development meeting your expectations as a remote or hybrid employee?

2. What adjustments to our current communication cadence might better satisfy your need for timely information and connection?

3. How well is your current level of visibility meeting your needs and supporting your development goals?

4. Which experiences and relationships are offering the most learning? What additional experiences and relationships might you like to explore?

5. Which systems and processes are supporting your growth?

6. How effectively am I sharing informal organizational information that you may not have easy access to as a remote employee?

7. Do you believe that your development opportunities are similar or equal to those of on-site employees?

8. What obstacles or challenges are getting in the way of developing at a distance?

9. What ideas do you have to improve your career development as a remote or hybrid employee?

Conversations like this model curiosity and an interest in growth. *Action* based upon them demonstrates and operationalizes your commitment. Don't let distance be a barrier to development.

What IF...

► **location didn't affect the quality or quantity of development employees enjoy?**

► **intention drove all discussions and decisions?**

► **we could create a virtual version of spontaneity and serendipity?**

CONCLUSION

KEEP MAKING A DEVELOPMENT DIFFERENCE

A lot has changed, but one thing is still the same. Leadership and your role in developing others remains a privilege, an honor, and a sacred responsibility.

Decades from now, people won't remember that you hit your numbers, met all your milestones, or came in under budget. People will remember that you made them feel valued, valuable, and capable. That you saw something in them that they may not have noticed. You'll be remembered for your care and attention, the opportunities you facilitated, and the confidence you enabled. How you helped others grow—that's a leader's true legacy and the most significant difference you'll ever make in business (and probably outside business as well).

Your career development efforts make more of a **difference** than you may ever know.

Building that legacy doesn't require sweeping initiatives. It requires simple but consistent actions that over time form a powerful development habit...if you keep at it. These are the conversations that organizations need and employees still want, so make sure you:

Keep the interview going. Continue learning about employees—and help them learn about themselves—throughout their careers. Genuine interest is too frequently in short supply, yet it goes a long way toward building loyalty, retention, and results. Using hindsight as a lens to understand who employees are and what they bring to the party in terms of skills, strengths, interests, values, and more will provide a solid foundation for development.

Keep a forward focus. Today's dynamic business landscape is affecting everyone's job. When you help employees develop the ability to scan the environment, anticipate trends, and spot opportunities, you provide a constructive context for development and future-proof careers.

Keep it real. Title- and role-based development is inherently limiting. No opening...no development. But if you can help employees recognize the limitations of the ladder and tease out what they want to do, you can help them move beyond the need to move.

Keep your eyes peeled. Find ways to bring development to life day in and day out. Waiting for an annual or prescheduled meeting to discuss career matters robs you and the employee of the energy and opportunities that are present always and everywhere. Pick up on cues to infuse development conversations into the workflow. Help others grow with the flow.

Keep it equitable. Make sure you're attending to the development of remote and hybrid employees just like you are for those who are on site—with a virtual twist and a whole lot of intention.

Career development is one of the most powerful and underutilized

levers

leaders have to drive engagement, retention, and **results.**

Keep the big picture in mind. Remember that you don't own talent; it's an enterprise-wide resource. Hoarding hurts everyone. Isn't it better to see a great performer move down the hallway rather than down the highway to a competitor? Develop a generous disposition.

Keep talking. Conversation is your most powerful tool to help focus, energize, inspire, and develop rich and satisfying careers—and to make the kind of difference that adds richness and satisfaction to your own career as well.

It's in your hands. When you help employees grow, you *keep* them—and you keep yourself from having to watch them go. So, keep it up. We're cheering you on.

What IF...

► you put just one or two ideas into practice with employees right now?

- -

They would **grow**,

    the *business* would **grow**,

        and so would *you*.

ACKNOWLEDGMENTS

This third edition would not have been possible without the thousands of readers who appreciated the value of career development and took a chance on the first two editions of *Help Them Grow or Watch Them Go*. Your feedback and insights have deepened our understanding of the topic and the evolving workplace within which development only becomes more critical.

The same goes for our clients, who allowed us the privilege of sharing these ideas throughout their organizations. Each consulting engagement, keynote presentation, and training session challenged us to consider the concepts and their application in new and different ways. We are grateful for your confidence and collaboration.

Sincere thanks go to the thousands of leaders and employees we've had the opportunity to cross paths with over the years. Your experiences, candor, and wisdom fill each page of this book as they've filled our hearts over the years.

And we can't forget about the foreign publishers who have made *Help Them Grow or Watch Them Go* available in Spanish, Portuguese, Japanese, Mandarin, Russian, and Farsi. Thank you for helping to spread these ideas, supporting development globally, and facilitating connections that make the world feel a bit smaller and warmer to both of us. We continue to deeply appreciate the "originals"—the team of colleagues and friends who contributed to the first edition. Ann Jordan, a longtime colleague of Bev's, lent her years of career development expertise, creative energy, and expansive thinking to the effort. Karen

Voloshin from DesignArounds was there from the very beginning, offering content, positioning, and her innate understanding of and focus on the leader. And we're more grateful than ever for our mutual friend, Judy Estrin, who brought us together in the first place.

None of this would have been possible without the urging and support of Steve Piersanti and the publishing team at Berrett-Koehler. When we write about exceptional leaders, Steve is our model. His authentic, straightforward, generous, curious, and humble style of leadership inspires those around him and sparks remarkable development and results. We're grateful to have been led by Steve and supported by Christy Kirk in marketing. Special thanks goes to our art director, Ashley Ingram, for her extraordinary creativity and commitment to realizing our vision.

We're most grateful to those closest to us who have helped us grow over the years. Team Giulioni has been in Julie's corner from the start. Peter, Jenna, Nick, and Diane have spent hours listening to half-baked ideas, sharing their experiences, and only rolling their eyes occasionally. Julie couldn't do all that she does without the exceptional contributions of Karen Voloshin, Brett Atkin, Jennifer Kuhlman, and Taryn Merrick. And special thanks go to every DesignArounds client who's partnered with us to advance this thinking.

Team Kaye was equally supportive. Facilitators and international associates, who presented the work worldwide, helped refine the message and brought specific feedback from the audiences they delivered to. Bev was supported by Jessica Brown, Kelly Graham, Linda Rogers, and Celeste Gonzalez, with the continued unwavering brilliance of Ann Jordan. And of course Barry, Lindsey, and Jill rooted for Bev whenever the going got tough. Barry accommodated Bev's scribbles in the middle of the night, and Lindsey and Jill were there for support each step of the way.

And finally, we acknowledge each other—two very different individuals with one very similar focus on development. Working together on both editions has helped us grow—so now we'll let you go.

INDEX

ABOUT THE AUTHORS

DR. BEVERLY KAYE

Dr. Beverly Kaye is recognized internationally as a professional dedicated to helping individuals, managers, and organizations understand the practical how-to principles of employee development, engagement, and retention. Her books and learning materials have stood the test of time. She was honored with the 2018 Lifetime Achievement Award from ATD (Association for Talent Development) and the 2018 Thought Leadership Award from ISA (Association of Learning Professionals) for her body of work. In 2022 i4CP (Institute for Corporate Productivity) presented her with the Industry Legend Award.

Beverly's contributions to the field of career development have been used by talent professionals for decades. She foresaw the effects of leaner and flatter organizations on individual careers and described a systems approach to building a development culture. She became an early game changer in an area of practice that had previously been only partially explored. *Up Is Not the Only Way* (2017) looked at career mobility and delivered an action-packed guidebook for employees and managers. It highlighted available career choices other than the traditional ladder. Her work in engagement and retention continued a commitment to offering practical strategies for today's workforce. The message in *Love 'Em or Lose 'Em* (2021) and its companion, *Love It, Don't Leave It* (2003), has been delivered to companies worldwide. *Hello Stay Interviews, Goodbye Talent Loss* (2015) was designed for managers who want to stem the tide of exit interviews.

Beverly leads a team of consultants and facilitators who deliver her messages globally. Bev is a Jersey Girl living in Sherman Oaks, California. She's been married for 50 years to her ex–rocket scientist husband, Barry, and is mom to two grown-up daughters, Lindsey and Jill.

JULIE WINKLE GIULIONI

Julie Winkle Giulioni is an author, speaker, trainer, and consultant who works with organizations and leaders to help them tap their most valuable competitive advantage: talent. Named one of *Inc. Magazine*'s top-100 speakers, Julie has traveled from Russia to China to Lithuania and beyond, helping leaders better develop, engage, and retain employees. She's a sought-after speaker because she consistently delivers creative insights as well as practical takeaways that change behavior. Julie's most recent book, *Promotions Are So Yesterday: Redefine Career Development, Help Employees Thrive* (2002), offers a research-backed framework for aligning employee interests with today's workplace realities and is a Nautilus and Axiom Business Book Award winner.

Julie's consulting firm, DesignArounds, works with Fortune 500 companies and organizations worldwide to develop and deploy bespoke learning experiences. Previously she was product development director at AchieveGlobal, held multiple training management positions, and was a professor and department chair at Woodbury University. She is a regular contributor to *Fast Company*, *SmartBrief*, and other publications and writes a regular column for *Training Industry Magazine*. Julie's work has been recognized by *Human Resource Executive Magazine*'s Top Ten Training Products, the New York Film Festival, the Brandon Hall Group, and the Global HR Excellence Council.

When Julie is not working with clients, she's active in her community, supporting efforts to address homelessness. A Southern California native, she's as comfortable doing stand-up paddle boarding as she is doing stand-up training. Julie currently lives with her husband, Peter, and they split their time between South Pasadena and La Quinta, California.

WORKING WITH THE AUTHORS

Bev and Julie each have their own independent companies that offer an array of specialized products and services. They came together to create this powerful book on developing talent through career conversations, and they partner often. Learn more about how time-starved managers can put the ideas from this book into practice. Access actionable tools. And explore AI-supported and other resources that will take your career development efforts to the next level. Visit help-them-grow.com.

BEV KAYE & CO.

Beverly Kaye founded Career Systems International more than three decades ago to offer innovative ways to help organizations solve their greatest talent challenges by engaging, developing, and retaining their people. Today Bev Kaye & Co. provides a comprehensive portfolio of award-winning learning solutions and services globally to a broad base of industries and organizations, including nearly two-thirds of the Fortune 1000 companies.

Conversations are the common thread and outcome for all of her

Our unique approach to organizational learning has always demanded solutions that are deceptively simple, delightfully engaging, deliberately flexible, and decidedly business-centric. These principles always guide us in developing and delivering solutions that provide high impact and measurable results.

areas of expertise. Simple but powerful, these critical conversations around engaging, growing, mentoring, and retaining talent ignite vital connections between employees, managers, and their organizations. Clients consistently report that they get powerful results as they create a strong voice for all their people in a surround-sound world.

Improving the business performance of our clients and the lives of all employees who seek to maximize their personal and professional potential is key to our offerings.

PRACTICAL SOLUTIONS

Career development. Career development consistently ranks as a top driver in employee engagement, not only impacting retention but also fueling an organization with innovative, productive, and impassioned employees. The CareerPower suite teaches employees to self-power their careers and teaches managers to act as a sounding board and career coach to drive the learning and growth of the individuals on their team. We offer webinars and learning solutions to support *Help Them Grow.* These solutions, offered in a variety of delivery methods, are highly interactive and provide assessments, tools, and activities to have managers and employees return to the job with actionable plans and the skill and confidence to hold meaningful development conversations.

Engaging and retaining talent. Engaging people and impacting business results requires managers to have a unique set of skills to effectively influence employee commitment. The learning solutions that support *Love 'Em or Lose 'Em: Getting Good People to Stay* provide today's leaders with the experience, knowledge, communication, and confidence to drive engagement worldwide. Though managers play a crucial role, employees can also take charge of their own satisfaction. *Love It, Don't Leave It* empowers individuals to create the conditions they need to improve job satisfaction without having to leave. As managers use the *Hello Stay Interviews, Goodbye Talent Loss,* engagement truly becomes a two-way street, and business results are maximized.

Consulting support. Our consultant team understands the importance of providing a strategic perspective to maximize business results for all of our solutions. We work to focus on an organization's culture, resource requirements, human resource structures, long-range goals, and business plans. The more our learning solutions are embedded in the larger system, the more impactful they can be.

Bev Kaye & Co., www.BevKaye.com, 818-995-6454

JULIE AND DESIGNAROUNDS

Julie Winkle Giulioni and her partner, Karen Voloshin, are cofounders and principals of DesignArounds, a bicoastal boutique learning and development firm committed to maximizing individual and organizational potential through bespoke learning experiences. Although their work spans the full range of leadership topics, Julie and Karen have a passion for bringing *Help Them Grow or Watch Them Go* concepts to life in organizations across the globe. DesignArounds's off-the-shelf and custom-designed learning experiences based on this best-selling book are the natural next step for leaders and employees who want to reconceive development in today's evolving workplace, build development into the daily workflow, and acquire the new skills required to engage in meaningful conversation and planning to support ongoing growth.

We're passionate about aligning learner needs, organizational outcomes, and cutting-edge learning strategies to deliver behavior change and bottom-line results. You can count on us for solutions that consistently captivate, resonate, and drive meaningful action...all designed around you.

We offer custom

► keynote speeches

► live and virtual instructor-led workshops

► e-learning

▶ microlearning via phone and text apps and more

▶ consulting and coaching

Train-the-trainer certifications allow internal facilitators to share the message within your organization. Julie, Karen, and other experienced DesignArounds facilitators are also available to deliver high-impact workshops and webinars.

But that's just the start of the journey. Embedding a development mindset and skill set in an organization requires a systems approach. The centerpiece of the DesignArounds system is the flexible e-Grow platform, filled with a tailored selection of content-rich, bite-size audio, video, text, and activity-based resources that turn new skills into long-term habits. Available on demand, e-Grow offers learners the tools they want, when they want them, to extend expertise, boost confidence, and realize results.

Julie Winkle Giulioni, www.juliewinklegiulioni.com, 818-219-7988

DISCUSSION GUIDE

Everyone has a favorite learning style and comfortable (and uncomfortable) ways to make change. Reading a book such as *Help Them Grow* is one way. For some, that's enough to get them to jump right in and start experimenting with new approaches. For others, learning happens more naturally and easily through face-to-face experiences, where concepts are taught and practiced. And for still others, learning comes through conversation—exploring ideas, opportunities, and approaches with peers who share their challenges and can support them in making changes.

This chapter-by-chapter discussion guide brings *Help Them Grow or Watch Them Go* to life. It's designed for use with two or more individuals who want to jointly consider the important topic of career development and how to make it happen in your organization.

This discussion guide is a flexible tool that you can use within the context of

► A one-on-one conversation. Schedule some discussion time with a colleague who has read the book and wants to take their understanding of it to another, more personal level.

► A staff or team meeting. Invite a team to read one chapter and dedicate time during the following meeting for a robust discussion.

► An online discussion. Post the questions on your shared site and invite an open electronic dialogue.

► Any other way that comes to mind.

Feel free to use all of the questions, or choose the ones you believe will spark the richest dialogue. Supplement this guide with your own ideas and questions.

The important thing is to begin the conversation and get people talking. Just like this book says, it all starts with a question. And you have plenty here.

Good luck, and please share your thoughts, successes, and the great questions you invent with us at our book website: help-them-grow.com (where you'll find lots of other helpful resources).

Chapter 1: Develop Me or I'm History!

1. At a Stanford graduation, Steve Jobs famously said,

> You've got to find what you love, and that is as true for work as it is for your lovers. Your work is going to fill a large part of your life, and the only way to be truly satisfied is to do what you believe is great work, and the only way to do great work is to love what you do. If you haven't found it yet, keep looking, and don't settle. As with all matters of the heart, you'll know when you find it, and like any great relationship it just gets better and better as the years roll on.

What is your reaction to this quote? What are the ramifications of not paying attention to what you love?

2. Let's take the financial issue off the table and assume employees are not looking just to benefit monetarily from taking on more responsibilities but are also searching for personal satisfaction in their jobs. What are some examples of times when someone invested in *your* job satisfaction? What can you learn from those examples to apply yourself?

3. Take apart the term *career development*. What is a career? What does it mean to you? Your employees? How about development? What does development mean to you? Has the meaning changed over the years?

4. What is the best forum to discuss goals and aspirations? Would your own preference be a private one-on-one discussion or an open-ended roundtable with lots of voices bouncing ideas off each other? What do you believe your employees want?

5. How often would you like to be approached by your manager to talk about your growth in the organization? Many companies seek this type of input from their employees once a year. Would you like to get together more often (quarterly, semiannually, or on an ad hoc basis) to discuss where you are now and how you can move forward? How would that change the nature of the conversations?

6. What's your own personal business case for helping others grow? (No party line, please!) What's the real "Why bother" in your eyes? If employees own their own careers, what's your role?

Chapter 2: Can We Talk?

1. Curiosity is a driving force in child development. As children we were all curious. What happened? Can a manager truly rekindle the flame of curiosity in employees? How and when was curiosity most recently ignited in you?

2. If we agree one of our goals is to help our employees grow, then cultivating true curiosity in our employees is as important for them as it is for us. How might you support their curiosity when it comes to the subject of careers?

3. It is said that A. J. Lafley, past CEO of Procter & Gamble, routinely asked himself and his team "What will you decide to be curious about on Monday morning?" How would you answer that question? How might you use this with your team?

4. What's your personal definition of career success today? How has it evolved over the past several years? How can you envision it evolving in the future? How would your employees define it? What in your organization's culture supports that definition? What plays against it?

5. Curiosity is a major impetus behind scientific discovery, possibly eclipsing the drive for economic gain. Why are we often more curious about our work (our science, our technology, our strategy) than we are about other people?

6. Describe your last career conversation with an employee. How did it go? What do you wish you had done? What do you think the employee might have wanted you to do differently? Might you have prepared differently?

Chapter 3: Let Hindsight Light the Way

1. How easy is it for you to describe your likes and dislikes at work? Can you name three in each category? Which is harder: identifying your likes or dislikes? Can you articulate what you find rewarding and what you find depleting in your professional life?

2. Ann Herrmann and Ned Herrmann, authors of *The Creative Brain*, (2015), said,

The urge to experience and define professional identity is a driving force that has motivated people throughout all history. In the search for some understanding of themselves, human beings repeatedly ask "Who am I? Why am I the way I am? Who can I become? In what direction should I go?" No one else can give us the answers. We need to find those answers for ourselves, and they seldom come up fast, simple or tidy.

Does this quote ring true for you? Why or why not?

3. People who feel fulfilled in life find the time to reflect about themselves and their challenges and opportunities. Given the pace of our lives, making time for reflection is now more difficult than ever for your employees. When do you stop and reflect? How might you model this in your current conversations?

4. Think about your own history for a moment. Who stands out as being most helpful in your own career growth? What did a manager or mentor do or say that made a difference to you? Do you think that kind of support is available now in your organization? Why or why not?

5. When people are asked about their weaknesses, they share them effortlessly. When asked to name their strengths, they often have difficulty and come up with a shorter list. Why might this be the case?

6. One of the most reflective questions a manager can ask is "And what did you learn from that?" Do you remember a time when someone asked you this question? What are some current projects or situations that offer you the chance to ask your team this question?

Chapter 4: Feed Me

1. How willing are you to hear honest feedback? What makes it easier? Harder? Do you know how each of your employees would answer that? How might you find out?

2. We often connect feedback with performance appraisals. Besides appraisals, what other opportunities can you use to provide feedback in a typical workday?

3. How comfortable are you conducting unscripted conversations with your employees who are seeking insight on how they are doing? Would you prefer having these conversations over video, on the phone, or face to face? Where are *you* most comfortable? Why?

4. Sam Culbert in *Get Rid of the Performance Review* suggests three profoundly simple questions: (1) What are you getting from me that you like and find helpful? (2) What are you getting from me (and/or the system) that impedes your effectiveness? (3) What are you not getting from me (and/or the system) that you think would enhance your effectiveness? Which one of these can you see yourself easily asking?

5. Is your organization's culture feedback-rich or feedback-poor? Can you give an example? Would you like to see it change? How?

6. Performance feedback is most often seen as a must-have in organizations of every size, and it is said to be the major differentiator between organizations that produce average results and those that outperform others. Do you believe this? How might your own performance feedback be more effective?

Chapter 5: What's Happening?

1. The late Harvard professor Clayton Christensen coined the phrase *disruptive innovation* and challenged leaders to think about what might knock their organization out of its current space. What disruptive innovations have you witnessed in your work life? What could disrupt your department? Your organization? How might you raise this with your employees?

2. Where do you go to learn about your competitors and what they are doing? What are some ways to challenge your employees to continually collect this information and share it with one another?

3. An employer's brand is a key part of what attracts talent to a particular organization. The right brand is a critical asset and a competitive advantage. What is your organization's brand promise about development? What brand promise are you making in your own department?

4. What professional webinars or conferences are most productive for you? Which would be good for your employees to attend? Can you make these opportunities happen? How might you or your employees share post-conference learnings?

5. An individual's capacity to tolerate internal and external pressures and adapt to these challenges is critical to life and career success. What is the most difficult work challenge that you've faced in your career? How did you deal with it? Looking back, what might you have done differently? How might you stimulate this conversation with your team?

6. We are indeed living in a VUCA world (old army term for "volatile, uncertain, chaotic, and ambiguous"). How is your organization, department, or profession facing a VUCA world? Which aspect of this is most difficult for you now? Which is most difficult for your employees? How might you create a forum for discussing this?

Chapter 6: If Not Up, Then What?

1. Do you understand what your employees really want from their careers? Life's challenges can propel us in very different directions as employees balance career growth and personal factors such as health and family in different ways. Describe a time when your personal life caused a change in your professional life, or vice versa. How can you be more sensitive to these instances in your employees' careers?

2. If success is in the eye of the beholder, then "up" may not be the only answer for everyone. How your employees measure their success

could be a critical insight for you. If you never provide a forum for this conversation, you might miss the opportunity to help them identify their next big career challenge. How might you initiate a conversation about perceptions of success?

3. Share the story of one of your career moves with others. When did you move laterally to explore another opportunity? Where did you take a step back to expand your perspective or retrench? When did you say "no" to a particular move? When did you opt for safety and security? What are some of your lessons learned? How can you share them?

4. All too often individuals leave an organization unaware of what career opportunities exist or what might have been possible. When have you seen your organization or department lose talent because of a perceived lack of opportunity? How could this be averted?

5. Have you ever been on a rock-climbing wall or watched others climb? What kinds of analogies come to mind as you think about moving from one position on the wall to another? Any words of wisdom? How might this relate to careers?

6. Which career mobility options seem most blocked in your organization? Check your assumptions with others. Where do you agree? Disagree? What's myth? What's reality? Have you opened a conversation like this?

Chapter 7: Same Seat, New View

1. OK, you want to inspire your employees but are hindered by today's leaner organizational structures. No fancy new titles and promotions allowed in this year's budget. Given this cost-restrictive environment, how can you provide challenging new ways for your employees to grow?

2. If it is the manager's job to reframe and revisit how employees visualize their jobs, there is benefit in helping them to expand their work to provide new opportunities. The simple act of exploring what else is possible breathes new life and new challenges into your employees' job. Think of a particular employee—what might you suggest?

3. If growth in place is the most accessible yet underused career development strategy available to managers, why aren't we taking advantage of it? How can managers encourage job enrichment without explicitly telling employees how to do this?

4. If what you do at work resonates positively with you, it will fuel your activity and enhance your experience. What would you like to explore? What are some of the different ways you can ask your employees that same question?

5. What does the saying "think globally, act locally" have to do with career development? Can you provide some examples from your own organization?

6. What cues or clues tell you that an employee has lost some spark and interest in their current assignment? What questions could you ask to test your assumption?

Chapter 8: Advancing Action

1. What has been your favorite way to learn? Give an example of something you recently needed or wanted to learn and how you went about it. Have you shared this with your team?

2. In what ways do you support employee learning opportunities? Do you believe your employees see you as supportive? How might you check this assumption?

3. How fluent do you feel in the language of experience-based learning? Beyond stretch assignments and special projects, what other organic opportunities might exist in your workplace that would allow employees to develop?

4. What best practices have you developed for creating flexible but effective development plans with your employees? What works? What doesn't?

5. What do you typically do to set an employee up for success before they engage in formal or informal learning? What else could you do to heighten their results?

6. What kinds of questions have you found to be most effective when following up on or unpacking a learning experience? Have any of your own managers asked you these questions? If they did, what impact did it have on your development experience? If they did not, how might asking these questions have changed your experience or cemented the learning?

Chapter 9: Grow with the Flow

1. What limits your ability to support the career development of your employees? Now, setting aside those limitations, what actions to help others grow are completely within your control? How easy is it to dismantle the limitations? For you? For your colleagues?

2. "Growing with the flow" is a mindset, an ability to stay present and observe the cues around you—and to use those cues to spark a conversation. What's challenging about doing this? What steps could you take to overcome those challenges? How possible is it to shift the current mindset of conversations happening only once a year?

3. Are you ready to have unplanned conversations with your employees? If you said "yes," congratulate yourself for honoring the cadence of business and the authentic, real-time, interactive nature of development. What is the easiest way for you to regularly infuse thoughtful observations and feedback into your conversations with your employees? If you said "no" to being ready, what is stopping you, and how can you overcome that?

4. What have you had to learn and relearn? What made the difference the second (or third? or fourth?) time around? What lessons do you take from this experience? Have you told that story?

5. Malcolm Gladwell described the role of a connector in his book *The Tipping Point*. How important are the connectors in your career? Have you acted as a connector to your employees? How might you do more?

6. What was the best stretch assignment you ever had? How—specifically—did it stretch you? What makes for a good stretch assignment? Think of one particular employee—what would stretch them? Could you help other managers with short-term stretch assignments for their employees in your department? What kinds of exchanges are possible?

Chapter 10: Developing at a Distance

1. Where do you fall on the debate over remote, hybrid, and on-site work? How are today's flexible working arrangements helping your organization, department, and employees? How might they be hurting each?

2. Consider the following statement from this chapter: "Unintentional inequity is a challenge for remote worker development." Why do organizations struggle with this, and what systems can be put in place to ensure equitable treatment and an even playing field?

3. Supporting the development of remote employees requires not just equal but greater intention in management practices. How can busy leaders make this effort sustainable?

4. How might the ritual of setting aside time at the beginning of virtual meetings for development discussions impact the dynamics of the meetings and relationships with employees?

5. The chapter suggests that leaders become cultural anthropologists and narrators. How might this approach be perceived by employees, and what boundaries should be maintained? What are the possible implications for authenticity? Privacy? Other concerns?

6. Which kinds of conversations (hindsight, foresight, insight) may take on even greater importance for virtual or hybrid employees? Why? Which might be more challenging to make happen virtually? How should leaders respond?

Dear reader,

Thank you for picking up this book and welcome to the worldwide BK community! You're joining a special group of people who have come together to create positive change in their lives, organizations, and communities.

What's BK all about?

Our mission is to connect people and ideas to create a world that works for all.

Why? Our communities, organizations, and lives get bogged down by old paradigms of self-interest, exclusion, hierarchy, and privilege. But we believe that can change. That's why we seek the leading experts on these challenges—and share their actionable ideas with you.

A welcome gift

To help you get started, we'd like to offer you a **free copy** of one of our bestselling ebooks:

www.bkconnection.com/welcome

When you claim your **free ebook**, you'll also be subscribed to our blog.

Our freshest insights

Access the best new tools and ideas for leaders at all levels on our blog at ideas.bkconnection.com.

Sincerely,

Your friends at Berrett-Koehler